advance praise for

THE SCHOOL CHOICE ROADMAP

"At a time when school choice is viewed through the lens of politics, Andrew Campanella offers a practical guide —underscoring the reality that for families, school choice is personal, not political. And with more school options than ever, this book should help parents navigate a complex landscape."

INGRID JACQUES, COLUMNIST, THE *DETROIT NEWS*

"An excellent book that will teach experts and parents something new. If enough people read it, the education system will be a little better for all."

JASON RUSSELL, THE *WASHINGTON EXAMINER*

"Andrew Campanella is one of the most passionate and knowledgeable voices in the school choice movement. *The School Choice Roadmap* is an essential guide for parents who want to find a learning environment where their children will succeed."

VIRGINIA WALDEN FORD, FOUNDER, D.C. PARENTS FOR SCHOOL CHOICE

"Finally, a tool that truly puts parents in the driver's seat when determining the best education for their child. Thank you, Andrew Campanella, for putting children and families first with a clear, easy to understand roadmap with no hidden agendas or bias."

WENDY HOWARD, FOUNDER, CELEBRATE YOUTH

"As a parent, this is the book I wish I had years ago as my family began our school choice journey. *The School Choice Roadmap* is a practical guide that will support parents as they navigate all their educational options and empower them to make informed education decisions."

TILLIE ELVRUM, PAST PRESIDENT, NATIONAL COALITION FOR PUBLIC SCHOOL OPTIONS

"Andrew Campanella is one of the rare people who can talk about education policy and school choice in a way that is understandable, empowering, and practical. *The School Choice Roadmap* is a valuable resource that will benefit countless families."

LISA GRAHAM KEEGAN, FORMER ARIZONA SUPERINTENDENT OF PUBLIC INSTRUCTION

"Parents are always looking for trustworthy educational resources to help them with their children. This book provides parents the educational, navigational tools needed to make informed decisions regarding their child's education."

CECILIA IGLESIAS, PRESIDENT AND FOUNDER, THE PARENT UNION

"*The School Choice Roadmap* empowers parents to choose the best school for their child and equips them with resources to take an active role throughout their child's education. In writing this book, Andrew Campanella has made a significant contribution to the educational freedom movement in our nation."

DEBORAH HENDRIX, EXECUTIVE DIRECTOR, PARENTS CHALLENGE

the school
choice
roadmap

the school choice roadmap

7 steps to finding the right school for your child

andrew campanella

BEAUFORT
BOOKS

First paperback edition January 2020

ISBN: 9780825309328 (paperback)
ISBN: 9780825308154 (ebook)

For inquiries about volume orders, please contact:
Beaufort Books
27 West 20th Street, Suite 1102
New York, NY 10011
sales@beaufortbooks.com

Published in the United States by Beaufort Books
www.beaufortbooks.com

Distributed by Midpoint Trade Books,
a division of Independent Publishers Group
www.midpointtrade.com
www.ipgbook.com

Book Designed by Mark Karis

Library of Congress Cataloging-in-Publication Data
Names: Campanella, Andrew, author.
Title: The school choice roadmap : 7 steps to finding the right school for your child / Andrew Campanella.
Description: First edition. | New York, NY : Beaufort Books, [2020] |
Summary: "Across the country, many parents today have more choices for their children's education than ever before. If you are starting the process of finding your child's first school-or if you want to choose a new learning environment-The School Choice Roadmap is for you. This first-of-its-kind book offers a practical, jargon-free overview of school choice policies, from public school open enrollment to private school scholarships and more. It breaks down the similarities and differences between traditional public schools, public charter schools, public magnet schools, online public schools, private schools, and homeschooling. Most importantly, The School Choice Roadmap offers a seven-step process that will help you harness the power of your own intuition-and your own expertise about your child's uniqueness-to help you find a school that reflects your family's goals, values, and priorities. The School Choice Roadmap is an optimistic, empowering book that cuts through the confusion in K-12 education-so that you can give your children every opportunity to succeed in school and in life"-- Provided by publisher.
Identifiers: LCCN 2019037813 (print) | LCCN 2019037814 (ebook) | ISBN 9780825309328 (paperback) | ISBN 9780825308154 (ebook)
Subjects: LCSH: School choice--United States. | Education and state--United States. | Schools--United States.
Classification: LCC LB1027.9 .C35 2020 (print) | LCC LB1027.9 (ebook) | DDC 379.1/11--dc23
LC record available at https://lccn.loc.gov/2019037813
LC ebook record available at https://lccn.loc.gov/2019037814

Manufactured in the United States of America

This book is dedicated to students and their parents. Every child in America deserves the opportunity to be happy and to succeed. School choice helps families achieve those goals.

contents

introduction

IN JANUARY 2013, I was walking into an education event in Kansas City, Missouri. I had recently started working in a new job—one that I will tell you about shortly—and I was scheduled to speak at this event about the importance of school choice. But before I could walk through the door, a woman and her young son recognized and stopped me. What they told me next changed my perspective on K-12 education.

The mother told me that she and her son were attending the event because she had recently searched for, and found, a different school for him. She was looking forward to sharing her experiences with other parents at the event. She was ecstatic that her son was finally succeeding in school. As inspired as I was by her remarks, it was what her son said that I will never forget.

"I finally feel like I belong somewhere," he told me, referring to his new school. "I don't feel like there's something wrong with me anymore. I am *happy* now."

There was something about the way that eight-year-old said the words, "I don't feel like there's something wrong with me anymore," that stopped me in my tracks. I asked the boy's mother to tell me more of their story. She shared that their family had moved to a specific neighborhood in part because they had heard that the community had a great elementary school. But once her son enrolled in second grade at that school, he was miserable. As a result, his grades plummeted, and his mother became distraught.

The boy was in a school that experts might define as high-performing or top-rated, but those accolades meant absolutely nothing to his mother once she realized that her son was struggling. When she enrolled him in another public school, however, everything changed. His outlook brightened, his grades improved and, as he told me, he felt like he belonged at his new school. He was finally happy.

I had worked in education policy since 2004, and I had talked with hundreds of parents about their experiences with their children's schools. But there was something about the discussion with this mother and son that felt completely different. For years, I had asked parents questions about school choice, and they had answered my questions. But what people tell you depends on what you ask them. The mother in Kansas City initiated the conversation. She and her son, not I, set the parameters of the discussion, starting that discussion by mentioning things that I might never have asked about: *happiness* and the feeling of *belonging*.

To them, school choice was not about finding a school that met a specific set of criteria that was defined by faraway experts. It was about one mom searching for, and choosing, a learning environment where her individual son could develop the confidence, joy, and feeling of belonging that empowered him to learn and succeed. The same is true for most families. Here is just one example: most parents *care* about a school's curricula and aggregate test scores, but what they are really *looking for* in a school or learning environment for their child is far more personal and complex than those factors alone.

After my conversation with that amazing mom and her equally amazing son in Kansas City, I started changing the way I talk about education. Frankly, I also stopped doing so much talking. Instead, I asked parents to simply tell me their stories. Then, I listened as families shared their hopes, dreams, and fears with me—absolutely incredible stories I never would have heard if I had asked specific questions. Using the same open-minded approach, I also asked school leaders and teachers to tell me their stories, too. What I discovered—about families and their experiences, and about the diversity and variety in K-12 education across our country—has inspired me.

In the years since, I have relied on that inspiration. I have used it, as best I can, to help families navigate the process of choosing schools and learning environments that meet the unique needs of their children. Thankfully, I have a solid platform to provide ideas and suggestions to parents who find this advice useful. But it is a platform I only reluctantly embraced just two years before meeting that mother and son in Kansas City.

MY OWN FEAR OF FAILING

In the spring of 2011, I sat down for lunch in Phoenix, Arizona, with my friend and mentor, Lisa Graham Keegan. I wanted Lisa's advice on a potential career change. It was an opportunity I was eager to pursue, but I was worried that I would fail.

Lisa is one of the most inspirational and effective leaders I have ever met. As an Arizona state legislator and the State Superintendent of Public Instruction, Lisa helped enact some of the first laws that created public charter schools. She has also worked to expand access to public and private schools for children across the country. Lisa views her work and life through a lens of unbridled optimism and positivity. I trust Lisa's advice, and the decision I was considering that spring day in Phoenix was important to me.

For seven years, I had worked in senior-level positions at nonprofit organizations focusing on K–12 education. In my first education job, I helped recruit teachers for public school districts. In my second position, I worked to promote and expand scholarship programs for children from low-income families.

The Gleason Family Foundation, a charitable organization, had recently invited me to take a new, full-time position helping to lead an education effort from the ground up. This effort, called National School Choice Week, would work with all types of schools and education groups to inform parents about the school choices available for their families. Tracy Gleason, the Gleason Family Foundation's president, helped create National School Choice Week because she felt that the national discussion about school choice was unnecessarily confusing to families, as it was often filled with jargon, acronyms, and buzzwords. She wanted to provide more opportunities for moms and dads to discover how school choice could benefit their children and their communities.

Tracy also recognized the need for a more inclusive approach to raising awareness about K–12 education, one that celebrated all types of schools and learning environments. She knew that among even the most effective national education organizations, most focused on promoting only one or two different types of schools. There were no national organizations that raised equal awareness of all schools and learning environments—from traditional public schools to public charter schools, public magnet schools, online public schools, private schools, and homeschooling.

National School Choice Week would fill that void and adopt a different and more user-friendly approach, including traditional marketing and public relations efforts, to reach moms and dads in communities across the country. It would also feature positive, local, and informational school choice events that would be planned independently by schools, home-school groups, organizations, and individuals. To make things more exciting and impactful, all of these efforts would take place during one big, fun week in January, and the National School Choice Week team would work year-round to help bring that week to life in a major way.

At the time of my lunch with Lisa, the first-ever National School Choice Week had just taken place. The week had been a success, with 150 events and activities having occurred across the country. Taking a full-time job with National School Choice Week sounded exciting. But I was worried. My new role would not just require me to sustain the excitement of that first year. It would also demand significant expansion of National

School Choice Week so that the effort could inspire as many families as possible.

As I told Lisa that warm day: I had a serious case of cold feet. "What if this fails?" I worried aloud. "What if I take a year-round job running an organization that focuses on one week of the year, and I am unable to grow or expand it?"

Lisa's response convinced me to think about things differently. "Yes, it could fail," she said. "But part of trying something new is to work as hard as you can to make it succeed. And if you do it right, it could be wildly successful and help a lot of people." I had been obsessing over the risks and the downside. Lisa helped me see the opportunities and the upside. I took the job.

GROWTH, DISCOVERY, AND THE NEED FOR A ROADMAP

In the years that followed, the National School Choice Week team worked to encourage schools, homeschool groups, organizations, and individuals to get involved and raise awareness about school choice in their own communities. Today, National School Choice Week is America's largest school choice public awareness effort and the world's largest annual series of education-related events. More parents search for "school choice" on Google during National School Choice Week than during any other week of the year. In January 2019 alone, our participants planned more than forty thousand school choice events and activities.[1]

The growth of National School Choice Week is inspirational, because it has shined a positive spotlight on the people who matter the most in education: students, their parents, and the amazing people who dedicate their lives to teaching children and running schools. And I get to meet so many of them!

Every year, I talk with hundreds of families. Like the conversation I had with the mother and son in Kansas City, many parents are excited to tell me that after searching for and finding the right school or learning environment for their child, their sons or daughters are not only learning, but happy and successful. Parents who actively choose schools or learning environments for their children are almost universally glad that they searched for, and found, the right educational fit. And almost as often, parents tell me that they wish they had started the school search process earlier. But some parents are nervous about pursuing the process, worried about asking the "wrong" questions, or simply afraid of failing.

Surprisingly, there are very few resources that provide tactical, practical advice for parents as they go through the process of selecting a school or learning environment for their child. In some areas, parent "navigator" organizations—like Families Empowered in Texas—work one-on-one with parents, at no cost, to help them pursue the school search process. However, there are only about a dozen of these organizations across the country.

Moms and dads frequently ask me for a school choice roadmap, one that they can use to better understand the similarities and differences between the six main types of schools—traditional public schools, public charter schools, public magnet schools, online public schools, private schools, and homeschooling. They also want a guide that will help them navigate the school search process so that they can find a school or learning environment that meets their child's needs and their family's goals.

THIS BOOK PUTS YOUR CHILD— AND YOUR FAMILY'S NEEDS—FIRST

I wrote this book to serve as the roadmap that so many parents told me they wanted. This book provides you with basic facts about the different types of schools that may be available for your child. Then, it offers you a step-by-step approach to finding a school or learning environment that truly meets your child's needs—an approach that lets your expertise about your child serve as your guide. Through it all, I have tried not to use any education jargon, so that this book is actually (hopefully) readable.

The advice in this book is intended to be helpful whether your child is just starting kindergarten or whether he or she is in elementary, middle, or high school. This book is practical, not theoretical. It is designed for:

- Parents who are about to enroll their child in school for the first time
- Parents who recently moved and need to find a new school for their child
- Parents who want their child to switch schools and find a better environment

In Part One, we will look at the school search process from a broad, goal-oriented perspective. We will talk about why choosing a school or learning environment can be helpful for your child's future. We will discuss how you, as a parent, are far more qualified to make decisions for your child's education than anyone else. I also provide information about the six different types of schools and learning environments. This will give you basic facts and general context before you start pursuing your school search.

Part Two focuses on the seven steps to choosing a school or learning environment for your child. These steps help you navigate the school search process by harnessing the power of your own intuition and the expertise you have as your child's greatest advocate. You will find several self-assessments, worksheets, and exercises in this section. These will help you to evaluate your own needs, your child's needs, and the different schools and learning environments that you are considering. Part Two also provides answers to frequently asked questions about school choice.

The Appendix provides a list of national resources that might be able to help you throughout the search process.

In writing this book, I relied on the advice, suggestions, and experiences of many of the same parents who asked me to write this book. These parents shared with me the lessons they had learned, the mistakes they had made, and the questions they wished they had asked during their own school searches so that I could provide a balanced, thoughtful school choice roadmap for other families. Throughout this book, you will hear from these parents. You will also have the opportunity to read some profiles of schools that I find particularly inspirational.

There are a few things this book will not do. First, this book is not political. I am not going to discuss the arguments for or against the different types of schools or make judgments about the quality of schools in specific areas. Each state has its own policies, and the availability of different types of schools varies in each city, county, and town. And just as every state and community has its own policies, your family has its own priorities.

You know your child better than anyone else on Earth, and you know your community better than I do.

This is also not a medical book, as I am not a doctor. Nothing in this book is designed to diagnose or treat any specific conditions that your child may have.

Finally, you will not get to the end of this book and find that I am subtly trying to prescribe a specific path for your child. I am not going to encourage you to choose one type of school over another. As you read, you will likely notice that I frequently refer not only to schools but also to learning environments. I use these terms interchangeably because I encourage you to consider all of your options—from schools with fixed locations to online schooling and homeschooling.

I am also not going to encourage you to follow the same path that I did. In fact, I am not a parent. One of the reasons why some parents shared their stories with me for this book is because they knew I could not judge them against, or compare their choices to, the ones I made for my own (nonexistent) kids.

So, this book is not political, medical, or prescriptive. It is about you, your children, and the schools or learning environments that you will select for them. In the end, I hope you will feel comfortable navigating the school search process. I hope you will feel empowered. I hope you will take the advice that Lisa gave me and not let the fear of failing prevent you from trying something new and exciting. Instead, work toward success. The result just might change your life—and most importantly, your child's life—for the better.

part one

AN OVERVIEW OF SCHOOL CHOICE AND THE TYPES OF SCHOOLS AVAILABLE

chapter 1

CHOICE IS POWERFUL, AND YOU ARE THE EXPERT

WE CHOOSE ALMOST EVERYTHING in our lives, and our lives are often defined by the choices we make. Some of the choices we make are monumental, like where to live, who to marry, and where to work. These choices can impact the totality of our lives. Many of our other choices are relatively minor, like what to eat for breakfast, what to watch on television, and how to spend our free time. These choices impact our daily lives.

By noon each day, we have already made dozens of decisions, some big and some small. Some of us make quick decisions. Some of us take our time. Regardless, we are constantly deciding what we like best, what interests us most, and what we believe is right for ourselves and our families.

As Americans, we know that having choices gives us more chances to build productive lives while aspiring to even greater success and happiness. Having and making choices is part of what freedom, liberty, and self-determination is all about, right?

But even in a society that was founded on the concept of individual choice, the notion of choosing schools still feels relatively new. For some families, it is exciting. For others, it feels daunting. And for a lot of parents, it's both. That is because in many states, school choice options are indeed new.

In the past, parents had fewer options for their children's education. They could send their kids to the traditional public school within their neighborhood or geographic zone. Or, they could opt to homeschool their children or pay private school tuition. For parents with no extra time or no money to spare, their options were severely limited.

Today, school choice is a reality for a record number of families in the U.S. Many families have more choices for their children's K-12 education than at any other time in history. That is because states and school districts are beginning to embrace a new approach to education, one in which parents have more freedom to customize their children's educational experiences.

For example, states are making it easier for parents to send their children to traditional public schools outside of their zones or districts. Most states are also empowering educators and community leaders to create unique public charter schools, public magnet schools, and online public schools—all of which are tuition-free. For families who want to choose private or religious education for their children, there are now more private and state-sponsored scholarship opportunities than ever before. For homeschooling families, there are more instructional resources and support networks available, along with policies allowing homeschoolers to participate in activities and sports at local public sector schools. We will get to descriptions of all of those terms, and types of schools, soon.

SCHOOL CHOICE IS ABOUT YOUR CHILD AND YOUR FAMILY

The expansion of school choice options has meant that more parents are checking out the different schools and learning environments available for their children. In fact, a record number of moms and dads in the U.S.—approximately one-third of parents with school-aged children—are actively choosing schools.[2]

School choice is not about specific policies or even specific types of schools, though. It is about the timeless value of *making choices*. Most importantly, it is about *your child*. School choice means making the decision to pair your child with a school or learning environment that best reflects his or her personality, interests, strengths, challenges, happiness, and creativity.

As you start the process of choosing a school or learning environment for your child, think about how you make other big choices in your own life. Think about how you would buy a car or find a house or apartment. Usually, you identify what you *need*. Then, you figure out how you can meet that need in a way that will benefit you the most. This is what you *want*. After that, you look at all of the *options* available. You narrow down those options, you weigh the pros and cons, you ask other people for their advice, and you make the best *decision* possible.

School choice is arguably more important than many of

the other choices you make, but the process of choosing is the same. Your child *needs* a quality education delivered in an environment where he or she will be successful. You *want* your child to learn in an environment that is best designed to meet his or her needs. There are hopefully lots of *options*—different schools and learning environments that you can consider so that you can find the right fit. You will narrow your choices down, talk to other people, ask lots of questions, and make a *decision*.

> *"I view a good education as a personal demand for freedom. A person's education level is often an indication of how successful they will be in society. Thus, having the ability to choose my child's education means I can make the best choices that will set him up for a free and successful life."*
>
> SHAUNETTE, A MOTHER FROM AIKEN, SOUTH CAROLINA

THE IMPORTANCE OF CHOOSING YOUR CHILD'S EDUCATION

But why is school choice so important, and how much will your child really benefit if you pursue this process?

In short, school choice can give your child a better chance at success and happiness. Choosing a school or learning environment for your son or daughter can lead to higher levels of learning and increased high school graduation rates.[3] Higher graduation rates mean that students earn more money over their lifetimes, are less likely to be incarcerated, and live longer.[4]

Parents who actively choose schools or learning environments for their children are more satisfied with their children's education, too. According to a study by the Institute of Education Sciences, parents who actively chose schools for their children expressed higher levels of satisfaction with the teachers in their child's school, the academic standards at the school, the school's approach to parental involvement, and the school's order and discipline than parents who did not choose or had no choices.[5]

In a way, that all makes sense. After all, one size doesn't fit all. Just think about your child and the other kids in your community. You will likely identify some similarities. But does your child have the *exact* same interests as the other children? Does your child learn in the *exact* same way? Probably not. Maybe your child acquires knowledge and information more quickly from technology than from books. Perhaps your child feels most comfortable when he or she is in a small group setting rather than a large group. Maybe your child has a really strong interest in science or writing but struggles with math. Or maybe your child has an interest that no other children in your community share. That's okay! In fact, all of these distinctions and differences are part of what makes your son or daughter unique and cool in his or her own right.

This uniqueness also helps explain why students respond in different ways to specific instructional methods and settings. What might be a perfect school for one student might not be a good fit for a child who lives right next door. Actively choosing a school or learning environment for your child allows you to select an education setting that best meets *your* child's unique interests. That decision can mean the difference between a child whose personality, quirks, talents, or struggles define him or her as "not fitting in" at school and a scenario in which those exact same traits fuel his or her momentum and development. Who among us doesn't want to fit in, feel valued, and be respected? Kids are no different.

Of course, a child's education does not take place in a

vacuum. School choice is not a magic wand. There are many things that can impact a child's development—from housing, to nutrition, to the unique issues that all families face. But a quality education, one that is tailored for your child's needs, can go a very long way.

Parents who actively chose schools or learning environments for their children rarely, if ever, regret pursuing the process. Certainly, a few parents may wish they had made different choices. But no moms or dads want fewer options. Instead, they tell me that the process of evaluating their child's needs, and considering the schooling options available to them, was absolutely worth it. In fact, most parents say they wish they had discovered school choice sooner.

> *"Not all children come with the same personalities, physical abilities, academic abilities, or talents. Being able to provide a child with the best educational option for his or her individual needs and abilities…is what makes school choice in America so important."*
>
> ISABEL, A MOTHER FROM BERKELEY, ILLINOIS

YOUR CHOICE CAN BENEFIT YOUR COMMUNITY

School choice does not just help individual students. It also helps schools and communities. When people talk about school choice, they occasionally talk about schools competing for students. Some people think that competition in education sounds too cutthroat, or that this competition is unhealthy for communities.

In reality, school choice is more complementary than competitive, because education is not a zero-sum game. Just as a community might have a variety of parks with different features and amenities to serve the unique recreational needs of its residents, communities can also have a variety of schools that meet the different and unique learning needs of its individual students. All types of schools can thrive in a community, creating a more diverse and interesting education climate—one in which more children are likely to succeed in school and thus are more likely to contribute positively to their communities when they grow up.

School choice encourages schools to continue enhancing the services they provide to students and families. Your choice of a school or learning environment for your child provides important information to school leaders and community leaders. That information should challenge these leaders to expand schools that parents and students find popular and effective and to improve schools that may not be meeting the needs of enough students. That type of thinking helps everybody.

School leaders say that having different types of schools in a community also promotes greater information-sharing between schools. A principal of a traditional public school recently told me that if parents find that their children are unhappy at his school, he works to address the challenges. But if his school is simply not a good fit for a particular child, he is relieved to have a list of other good schools and learning environments so that the parents of that child can find a better fit.

"Education is not only about science, math, and the core subjects. It's about being a humanitarian and coming out of your box. It's about how to relate to the society that you are living in by making a change, and to give ten times more than you are taking. It is about being able to appreciate life and the opportunities in life."

ELIZABETH ZAHDAN, CEO AND FOUNDER, BRIGHT HOPE
ACADEMY CENTER, NEW YORK, NEW YORK

NEVER FORGET THAT YOU ARE THE EXPERT

School choice truly changes lives. But throughout the process of evaluating your school choice options, you may encounter some confusion and frustration. When and if you do, please remember that *education can be confusing to everyone*. In fact, my introduction to the world of education policy started out with a lot of confusion.

The year was 2004. One day, as I was scrolling through job postings on the internet, I came across a position at an organization that helped recruit teachers for public school districts. I was far from an education policy expert. My only professional experience in education was volunteering in an after-school YMCA program that helped students learn more about civics and government. Even so, I applied for the teacher recruitment job. One of the interviewers sensed that my knowledge was lacking. "Tell me what you know about education policy," she said.

I spoke from the heart about the students I met at the YMCA program and their struggles with literacy. I told the interview panel that, while I was not an expert on education, I cared about the issue and had the capacity to learn. I got the job, not because I pretended that I knew more than I did, but because I was honest about what I did not know. And I showed that, above all, I cared about the organization's goals. It must have worked, because I was offered the job, accepted it, and immediately started learning.

Our organization recruited talented professionals to change careers and become public school teachers. We tried to get doctors to become science teachers, bankers to become math teachers, and journalists to become English teachers. As we started reaching out to people, we quickly realized that even the most enthusiastic prospective teachers got frustrated by the jargon and complexity surrounding education.

If you are nervous about starting the school search process, or if you worry that there is *too much that you do not know,* do not fear. You have a secret weapon in your information arsenal: the fact that you know your child better than anyone else on this planet. As a parent, you understand your child's interests, potential, strengths, and weaknesses better than anyone. Nobody cares more about your child than you do. Nobody has a greater stake in your child's happiness and success than you. That means that you are truly *the expert,* and nobody is more qualified than you are to make decisions for your child's education.

Every parent can navigate the education system simply by being direct, honest, and persistent about the things they do not know. It does not matter where you live, how many years you spent in school, or how much money you make. *You can do this!* When you encounter something that seems overly complicated or utterly bizarre, just ask for as much clarification as possible. Nothing in education is too hard for any of us to figure out once we cut through the education-speak.

As you pursue the school search process, you may also encounter people—friends, other parents, or people who work in education—who may tell you, or who may insinuate, that you are making "the wrong choice." When you encounter these people, I encourage you to smile, nod, and continue on your path of choosing the right school or learning environment for your child. Other people may have opinions, but you have the experience, you have the facts, you know your child, and you are the expert. Trust yourself.

Chances are, you have big dreams for your child. Think

about those goals and aspirations throughout every step of this process. In fact, to succeed in this process and find a school or learning environment that meets your child's needs, you will need to place those values at the forefront of your mind. Never let them get squeezed out by the countless facts, processes, procedures, and terms you will hear along the way. Never let your concern, care, and love for your child get overshadowed by fear or doubt.

> *"Do not be intimidated by those afraid of change but stand firm on what is best for your children."*
>
> ZETA, A MOTHER FROM DEVILS TOWER, WYOMING

> *"Consider your child's needs and your family's situation. Don't assume that the best choice for your neighbor's or sister's child will be the best for your child. Don't be afraid to make a change if your original choice isn't working. You are your child's best advocate!"*
>
> LYNNE, A MOTHER FROM LEHI, UTAH

> *"Do what works best for your individual family, not what society thinks is best. Each child is unique and learns at his or her own pace. Focus on what matters most and what is exciting and interesting...and you can learn together."*
>
> ALICIA, A MOTHER FROM SEVIERVILLE, TENNESSEE

Finding a school that your children will love

Kiyomi and Grace love their school. On a spring day in 2019, these fifth graders from Albuquerque, New Mexico were on the edge of their seats, eagerly waiting to find out which of their school's academic teams had won a school-wide competition.

All of the students at their school, the New Mexico International Academy, participate in the competition, which includes academic exercises and other activities so that the strengths of all students can be considered. The winning team is awarded the *Copa de Campeones*—the championship trophy.

For Kiyomi and Grace, the competition is not the only reason that they are happy at school. Their classes are exciting, too, and they are grateful for their teachers.

"We have a lot of special classes. We have an amazing art teacher. We have music. We play the violin. We do Aikido, which is a martial art," Grace says. Both students are also bilingual and biliterate in English and Spanish, as well as proficient in Arabic. Language and cultural immersion are at the core of the academy's educational approach.

"I think that it is really cool to learn more languages than what you did know," Kiyomi says. "I started off with English, and then from kindergarten through fourth grade, I learned a lot more Spanish, and I'm taking Arabic now." Grace wants to eventually become a teacher. Or possibly, an Olympic swimmer. Kiyomi says she hopes to pursue acting and singing.

Todd Knouse helped to create this tuition-free public charter school and now serves as its principal. I asked him how it was even possible for students to master both English and

Spanish and become proficient in Arabic by the fifth grade—and have so much fun in the process. "It sounds almost magical, and that is the power of starting language immersion when children are in kindergarten or even younger," he says. That immersion includes teaching many of the school's classes in Spanish and a variety of in-school and after-school clubs and activities so that all of the school's classes are connected. "We try to create experiences for our students, so that they can see the connections that happen in real life and outside of school."

Soon, even more students in New Mexico will have the opportunity to enjoy the experiences provided by New Mexico International Academy. The school is expanding next year so that other students can discover the same love of learning that is inspiring Kiyomi and Grace.

"No one comes to New Mexico International Academy because they have to. Everybody is here because their parents said, 'I like the mission of that school. We're here because we want to be here,'" Knouse says. "It makes the administration responsive to the needs of students and parents."

Regardless of where your family's school search takes you, your child deserves a learning environment that can inspire the same love of learning that makes Kiyomi and Grace so motivated and happy.

chapter 2

SCHOOL CHOICE 101: THINGS TO KNOW BEFORE YOU START YOUR SEARCH

MOST PARENTS IN AMERICA have more choices for their children's education today than at any other time in history. By choosing a school or learning environment for your daughter or son, you will join the ranks of millions of moms and dads who have made choices designed to meet the needs of their children.

Before you begin the process of searching for the school or learning environment that will meet your child's needs, it is helpful to survey the landscape and discover the different types of schools that might be available in your community.

Broadly speaking, there are six main types of schools and

learning environments in the U.S. These schools share similarities, but they also have key differences. In the next several chapters, you will read more about each type of school, so that you can understand how different schools are managed, what makes them unique, their admissions policies, whether they charge tuition, and what type of transportation you can expect. Here is a quick overview:

- **Traditional public schools** are run by school districts and do not charge tuition. In most cases, students do not need to take tests to get accepted into traditional public schools. Some states allow parents to choose any traditional public school in their district. Other states allow parents to send their children to traditional public schools in other districts, too.
- **Public charter schools** are run by organizations and do not charge tuition. Students do not need to take tests to get accepted into public charter schools. What makes charter schools different from traditional public schools is that they have more flexibility in trying out unique instruction methods and approaches to education.
- **Public magnet schools** are run by school districts or groups of school districts and do not charge tuition. Magnet schools teach all academic subjects to students, but these schools are focused on specific themes like math, science, technology, writing, or performing arts. Some magnet schools require students to take tests for entry, but most do not.
- **Online public schools** are usually run by state governments, school districts, or charter schools. Online public schools do not charge tuition, and students do not need to take tests to get accepted into them. At online public schools, students use

computers at home to learn from teachers via the internet.

- **Private schools** are run by organizations or religious entities, and they charge tuition. There are many different categories of private schools. Some, but not all, private schools require students to take tests before being accepted to attend. Many states now offer state-sponsored scholarship programs to help cover tuition costs, in addition to scholarships offered by individual schools and local scholarship organizations.

- **Homeschooling** is the process of educating your children in the home. Each state has different rules and policies regarding homeschooling, but parents in every state have the right to teach their children in the home.

In addition to learning more about how each of these types of schools are run, the next few chapters will provide you the opportunity to hear from teachers, school leaders, parents, and even some students in these schools. You can also read profiles of schools that I find inspirational. Of course, not every school will resemble or mirror the practices, techniques, and strategies of the schools I have chosen to profile. As you will soon discover—and likely know already—education is filled with diversity and variety. For families, that means more choices and opportunities.

> *"Look for what works for your children, what works for your family. We are fortunate, these days, that we can choose what's best for us. No choice is the wrong choice. The beauty of having options is in itself the best choice."*
>
> MAYDA, A MOTHER FROM MIAMI, FLORIDA

SCHOOL CHOICE OPTIONS INCREASED
BECAUSE AMERICA'S ECONOMY CHANGED

Before we get into the details about the six different types of schools, let me offer a quick (and optional) history lesson on why many of these options exist today when, just a few short decades ago, most parents had far fewer choices for their children's education.

Years ago, if students went to their zoned public schools and succeeded, they could often go to colleges or into professions or trades. But even if students did not do particularly well in school, many young people could find decent, middle-class jobs in their communities. As international competition and free trade expanded, things changed. Young people discovered that it was harder to land those decent, middle-class jobs. Students found that they were competing for work with people in other countries, and some jobs left the U.S. entirely. Meanwhile, U.S.-based jobs increasingly required higher skill levels. As companies automated their processes and came up with computerized ways to do things, their employees needed to be able to operate machinery that was more complicated than ever before.

The U.S. truly confronted these challenges for the first time in 1983 with the publication of a federal study titled, *A Nation at Risk*. Commissioned by President Ronald Reagan and the U.S. Department of Education, the report offered a major warning: "Our once unchallenged preeminence in commerce, industry, science, and technological innovation is being overtaken by competitors throughout the world," it said. The report called for greater educational opportunities so that all Americans could "stretch their minds to full capacity, from early childhood through adulthood, learning more as the world changes itself."[6]

That is eventually what happened in many states after parents demanded more options.

In the early 1990s, educators and state policymakers across the U.S. responded to the needs of families and created groundbreaking new programs to provide more choices in education. In Minnesota, for example, a group of public school teachers banded together to create the nation's first public charter school with bipartisan support from state lawmakers.[7] In Wisconsin, another bipartisan team of educators and elected officials worked with parents to create a scholarship program so that children from low-income families could attend private schools in the city of Milwaukee.[8] Those early programs were just the beginning. Today, most states offer public charter schools,[9] and more than half offer some form of publicly supported private school scholarship or tuition assistance program.[10]

Traditional public schools also innovated and improved to meet the nation's needs. Educators and state lawmakers in many states listened to moms and dads and relaxed their boundaries, or zones, to allow parents to have more choices within traditional public school systems. These programs, often referred to as open enrollment, or public school choice, are now available in some form in almost every state.[11]

Public school districts also started expanding magnet schools and magnet programs. Magnet schools were originally conceptualized as a way to accelerate school integration. As the demand for educational options grew, magnet schools embraced theme-based learning, while retaining their focus on diversity—so that districts could provide even more public-sector school choices.

As more families began connecting to the internet in the late 1990s, education reached yet another milestone. In

1997, a teacher launched the first-ever statewide, full-time, tuition-free online public school in Florida.[12] Today, full-time, tuition-free online public schools are available in more than half of U.S. states.[13]

Meanwhile, the demand for educational opportunities led to a greater interest in homeschooling. In the 1980s and 1990s, moms and dads led successful fights to change laws in states that had previously made life difficult for homeschooling families.[14] These supporters also built strong networks and support groups to provide resources to homeschoolers. The result was a dramatic increase in the number of students receiving education in the home.[15]

Over just three decades, American education has changed significantly thanks to collaboration between parents, teachers, school leaders, and policymakers. These changes have provided an enormous benefit to children and families. They have built an environment where the variety of choices and options has begun to mirror the choices we have in every other aspect of our lives. Most importantly, the increasing diversity of choices is finally beginning to reflect the diversity that makes our country so unique.

"Choice is a very American thing. Our founders came over here because they wanted choice. They wanted to go somewhere where they had the freedom to choose. That was the very genesis of our country. I think choice in education is an absolute. You cannot be stuck in a place where you are told, 'This is where you go to school, and you have no choice about it.' That is not joyful."

DEBBIE BEYER, FOUNDER AND EXECUTIVE DIRECTOR, LITERACY FIRST CHARTER SCHOOLS, EL CAJON, CALIFORNIA

A GREAT SCHOOL OR LEARNING ENVIRONMENT
IS ONE THAT WORKS FOR YOUR CHILD

With the growth in school choice options, there is understandable curiosity about whether one type of school is better than another. In fact, almost every week, someone asks me which *type* of school is the best choice. People want to know if charter schools are better than traditional public schools. They want to know if private schools are better than charter schools. These are totally reasonable questions.

I value honesty and candor. If I had an answer to this question that was definitive, I would share it with you. But chances are, we do not live in the same community. Your community has different options than mine. You know, better than I do, whether the schools in your area—regardless of type—provide an effective education for some, many, or most children. What's more: I probably haven't met you or your child, and I do not know your child's needs, interests, strengths, and challenges. You do.

The truth is: I do not believe that one type of school is better than another type of school for *all* students. The best school or learning environment is the one that works best for your *individual child,* based on the options available in *your individual community.* School choice is not about making one big choice for all kids everywhere. It does not mean picking one type of school that should, or will, work perfectly for every child. Instead, school choice is personal. It means millions of individual parents, in thousands of unique communities, make individual choices for individual children.

For your family, that choice might be a traditional public school. Or, it could be a public charter school, a public magnet school, an online public school, a private school, or homeschooling. I regularly work with schools and learning environments of all types, and I can think of so many examples of inspirational, exciting schools in each category.

As you pursue the school search process, I encourage you to develop your own definition of what a *good school* is, or should be, for your child. Here's why: imagine if everyone in a community thinks one particular school is incredible, but your child attends the school and is struggling there. What use does the *good school* label do for you? It is cold comfort knowing that your child attends a *good school* and is still having troubles. So many parents hesitate to take action or consider different schools for their children because their child's current school is highly regarded in their community. As a parent, it is up to you to decide whether a school meets your child's needs. Part Two provides a variety of methods and techniques that you can use to do just that.

"School choice allows us to make the best decision based on the needs of our children. We are able to have our child go to a school that allows him to grow and thrive. Our child went from failing and being left behind to succeeding and being on track for college. He is graduating at the top of his class. School choice has helped him to be successful."

ROBERT, A FATHER FROM LAKE WORTH, FLORIDA

FOR SOME FAMILIES, SCHOOL CHOICE MEANS MULTIPLE LEARNING ENVIRONMENTS

If you have more than one child, school choice also gives you the opportunity, if you wish, to select a different school or learning environment for each of your children. That is exactly what an increasing number of families across America are doing. These *multiple-choice* families underscore the importance of focusing on each child's needs rather than just zeroing in on the *types* of schools under consideration.

Erica Cox is one of these parents. Erica and her husband live in California. They send their seventeen-year-old son, Dominic, to a public charter school. Their fifteen-year-old daughter, Abigail, attends a private school that focuses on the performing arts. And Erica homeschools their twelve-year-old daughter, Zoe.

For Erica, sending her three children to three different schools was not always in their family's plans. "I started off never thinking this would ever happen," she says. "But if you want your kid to be a successful student, you need to find the right type of school and environment for him or her to thrive in. Don't assume because it works for one child, it will work for the others.

"I would not change anything of where my three kids are right now," Erica says. "They are all in the perfect spot for them, and I'm very happy with the choices we made. Some are hard, some require sacrifices, but my kids know that they are in the best possible spot for them to succeed."

"I am a mom of eight children and believe me, they are all different in their education levels and personalities. I have had to choose different schools for two of them. But in the end, it was the right choice for us."

ELLEN, A MOTHER FROM MORRISON, COLORADO

JUST AS EVERY CHILD IS UNIQUE, EVERY SCHOOL IS, TOO

As you prepare to embark on the school search process, please remember that every school is indeed unique. Categorizing schools into six broad sectors or types—traditional public,

public charter, public magnet, online public, private, and home—has some limitations. The six types of schools are categorized based on the ways they are managed and run, but within each sector, you will find many different approaches to education.

For example, just because a school meets the definition of a traditional public school does not mean it will look or feel the same as another traditional public school. After all, your neighborhood public school should be designed to reflect your neighborhood, not someone else's. In a single day, you could talk to two traditional public middle school principals in the same city and find out that one school focuses on rigorous academic instruction while the other has a more relaxed atmosphere, yet both get great results from the majority of students they serve.

The same is true for all types of schools. One charter school might have a completely different educational approach than another, as each of these schools is based on the unique educational strategy designed by its founders. Magnet schools all focus on themes, allowing for thousands of distinct schools with themes ranging from science and technology to the performing arts and beyond. Diversity within the private school sector is expansive, including everything from independent schools to schools that offer Catholic, Christian, Jewish, and Islamic faith-centered education. Online schools are different, too, with some schools focusing on a more structured school day and others offering a more flexible schedule. Within the homeschooling community, there are different philosophies, curricula, and ideas on how best to educate children.

Just as each school within each type is unique, no one type of school has a monopoly on some of the most popular educational approaches, services, and instructional strategies, either. For example, an increasing number of families are seeking vocational or career and technical education for their children. You will find schools of all types that focus on this approach. Or, perhaps you may have heard of Montessori education. There are schools of all types that either adopt Montessori-style curricula or classify themselves as Montessori schools. An increased interest in science, technology, engineering, and math (STEM) has led more schools of all types to provide enhanced focus on these subjects, too.

> *"When we're working with students who have a lot of trials in life before they get to school, we try to make our school a positive environment where they can be themselves, but also understand that structure is necessary. We give students permission to be creative, but also to be kind. It's very important to us to have teachers who are caring and concerned about our students and will push them to learn as much as possible but will also help them along the way."*
>
> DR. TARCIA GILLIAM-PARRISH, ADMINISTRATOR, SHELBY
> COUNTY PUBLIC SCHOOLS, MEMPHIS, TENNESSEE

SCHOOL CHOICE REALITIES

The fact that more parents in the U.S. today have choices for their children's education is a good thing. The increased diversity and variety in K-12 education is exciting, too. But before you read about the different types of schools that might be available, here's a tough reality that I want every parent to know: the choices available for your family depend almost entirely on where you live.

That is because every state has different school choice policies. The legislatures and governors of states decide whether to allow open enrollment programs for traditional public schools, whether to allow charter schools, and whether to establish online public schools. State leaders also decide whether your state will offer a state-sponsored tuition assistance program for private schools. State leaders also decide how much they want to regulate homeschooling families.

The state in which you live is not the only location-specific factor that will impact the choices you have, though. Where you live within that state can also make an enormous difference. For example, if you live in a largely rural area, you may find that you have fewer nearby school options than if you live in a suburban or metropolitan area.

Individual school districts can also determine how many options are available. In some states, school districts have a say in whether charter schools can open. In most states, school districts decide whether to open public magnet schools, too.

The result is that in some states—and in specific areas within those states—parents will find that their children have more overall choices than in many other places. Arizona and Florida are good examples of this. Both states offer an abundance of school choice options for families. But at the opposite end of the spectrum, unfortunately, are states like North Dakota and West Virginia. These states may have schools that many families love, but they do not offer much flexibility for parents.

In reality, most states have policies that fall somewhere in between. You are likely to discover that you have some choices, but perhaps not the full menu of options that you might want. As you read more about the different types of schools available across the country, you should take some time to discover the options in your state. The upcoming chapters provide snapshots of state-by-state school choice policies. In addition, you can find other resources related to your state's school choice policies this book's website at schoolchoiceroadmap.com.

> *"School choice is everything! I watched my parents fight for my education, and now school choice allows me to provide my children with an excellent education, so that they can thrive."*
>
> LEAH, A MOTHER FROM PHOENIX, ARIZONA

CHOOSING TO SWITCH SCHOOLS

Some of you reading this book will be choosing your child's first school or are planning to move to a different community. Some of you, however, may be reading this book because you want to choose a different school for your child. Perhaps you feel that your child is unsafe, is not learning, or is unhappy in his or her school. Regardless of your reasons, there is no wrong reason to consider options that might work better for your family.

But perhaps you are not sure whether changing your child's school or learning environment is a good idea. Parents frequently ask, "When should I work to fix a problem at my child's school, and when should I look for a different option?" People are often reluctant to overreact, or they worry that switching schools might do more harm than good for their children.

Trust your intuition! If your intuition is telling you that you should address a problem at your child's school and that switching schools would be too disruptive, listen to yourself. At the same time, if your intuition is telling you that your child is not in the right school or learning environment, it is time to evaluate your options.

Of course, if you feel that your educational radar might

be a bit rusty and you cannot figure out what your intuition is telling you, that is okay. Part Two includes several exercises, beginning on page 121, that will help you identify what you are looking for in your child's school or learning environment. If your child's current school is not addressing the items that you rank as your priorities, it is likely time to look elsewhere.

Every situation is different. Remember that you can still evaluate different schools and learning environments while trying to improve things at your child's school. In the Frequently Asked Questions chapter at the end of Part Two, you will find suggestions for addressing problems at your child's school.

If you choose to move your child from one school to another school or learning environment, please know that other parents might try to dissuade you from making a change. This happens frequently. Remember: you need to make the best decision for your child and your family, and you have the intuition and expertise to make those decisions. If people ask, simply explain that your decision is personal and that, while other families might have positive experiences with a school, you need to find a different option for your son or daughter.

> *"School choice has meant a very positive outcome for my daughter. She has been able to advance one and a half years ahead of schedule and continues to soar. My daughter was bullied in her former school because she was an intelligent girl who excelled in math. School choice rocks."*
>
> MARY, A MOTHER FROM YORK, PENNSYLVANIA

DISCOVERING THE SIX TYPES OF SCHOOLS

Making a choice for your child's education can provide positive and lasting benefits to your child, your family, and your community.

Now, it is time to dig deeper and discover more about the different types of schools and learning environments available. These school types have similarities and differences. In the following chapters, you will read about traditional public schools, public charter schools, public magnet schools, online public schools, private schools, and homeschooling.

You are more than welcome to read these chapters in one sitting, reference them later, or skip them entirely. You won't hurt my feelings—because, really, I will never even know you skipped anything. So, if you're up for it, let's get started!

"Listen to your child and be involved. What works one year, may not the next. What works for one child, may not work for another."

RACHEL, A MOTHER FROM LANSING, MICHIGAN

"Listen to your gut. Ask all the questions even if you believe they are silly. Nothing is silly when it comes to finding the perfect fit for your children, your family, and your life."

KATIE, A MOTHER FROM AIKEN, SOUTH CAROLINA

"It's fundamental for families to be able to select the schooling of their choice. Children are not generic. They have specific strengths and weaknesses. These core attributes are what makes a blueprint for their future. Being able to access what they need and when they need it, developmentally, can secure their future success."

LESLIE, A MOTHER FROM HOUSTON, TEXAS

One amazing mom saw an unmet need, so she built a school

Robin Sweet searched tirelessly for a school that would serve the needs of her son. Her family visited schools in their Arizona hometown, talked to administrators, and still came up empty. She could not find a school that provided a specialized learning environment for students with Asperger syndrome.

Students with Asperger syndrome have unique needs. They tend to be academically gifted, but they struggle in social and interpersonal situations. "For these kids, because they're bright, they're aware," Sweet says. "These are the kids who are bullied, teased, and tortured, not just in an academic environment, but in life. Life is not easy, and people are not always going to be kind. The loveliness of this population is they believe everybody's good."

Sweet believes that to effectively address these needs, a school should measure success by looking not just at student achievement but also whether students are prepared to successfully enter their adult lives.

Without a good option for her son, Sweet opened Gateway Academy near Phoenix, Arizona in 2005 to serve students with exceptional needs. Gateway is a private school with an eight-acre campus. The school uses equine therapy, occupational therapy, and support services for children with Asperger's. It also offers a music therapy program that encourages students to work together, learn, and have fun. "Each class has their own rock band, which is priceless," Sweet says. "They all learn how to play acoustic guitars, electric guitars, drums, keyboards, percussion instruments, and vocals. They learn how to read music and then, at the end of the year, we have a rock concert for the community."

Sweet's work is extraordinary. Her compassion is endless. And the results speak for themselves: 100 percent of Gateway's graduates go to college. But without Arizona's state-supported private school scholarship program, it is unlikely that many Gateway families would be able to choose this school. "Ninety-eight percent of our student population is funded by the Empowerment Scholarship. These families would never, ever be able to afford a private school that is specialized to support their child otherwise," Sweet says. "I can't even talk enough about how powerful and meaningful it is to these families."

Today, Sweet's son is twenty-six years old. He has two college degrees. As Sweet puts it, "He's found himself." Thanks to Sweet's love and determination, Gateway Academy will continue to help other students find their own paths in life.

chapter 3

TRADITIONAL PUBLIC SCHOOLS

THE BASICS

Parents in every community across the U.S. can send their children to traditional public schools. These schools are managed by school districts, governed by local school boards, and charge no tuition for children to attend.

There are more than 90,000 traditional public schools across the U.S.[16] With the exception of selective public schools, traditional public schools must accept all students, regardless of their academic performance or needs.

YOUR CHOICES

Many children are assigned by their school districts to attend traditional public schools based on their community, neighborhood, or school zone. This process is called public school assignment. Many states, however, now offer parents more flexibility to choose traditional public schools outside of their zones. In some areas, parents can choose any traditional public school in their district. Other states allow students to attend traditional public schools in any district.

These policies are known as open enrollment. You may also hear these programs referred to as public school choice, inter-district school choice, or intra-district school choice. Half of U.S. states require school districts to participate in some type of open enrollment program.[17] The most common limitation that states place on many of these programs involves space and availability. Students can usually only transfer to another traditional public school if the chosen school has not reached capacity.

> My Take: Many traditional public schools can
> be far from "traditional" and often offer unique
> programs tailored to their communities

I spent my entire elementary and secondary education in traditional public schools and had a very positive experience. But before I started working in education, I had almost no idea how much diversity and variety existed within and among traditional public schools. As one teacher recently said, it is almost unfair to call many schools *traditional* because they often carefully tailor their courses and activities to complement the needs of their communities.

Two schools that illustrate this trend are Coyote Springs Elementary School in Prescott Valley, Arizona and De Zavala Elementary School in Houston, Texas.

At Coyote Springs, the school not only provides instruction in all of the traditional academic subjects; it also works to build student knowledge and skills in five important areas that it calls the *Five Cs:* critical thinking, creativity, collaboration, communication, and community connections.

According to the school's principal, Candice Stump, Coyote Springs developed those principles in collaboration with parents, community stakeholders, and area businesses. One way that school leaders bring all of those principles together is by working with students to plant and cultivate a school garden, which includes dozens of fruit trees. That garden provides a springboard for students to learn math, reading, social studies, and entrepreneurship—and is a complement to the school's suburban and rural surroundings.

"As a school community, we have taken on the work of knowing that we're preparing kids for futures that have not yet been determined," Stump says. "Our team of educators always needs to make sure that our school gives students the opportunities that they need to be successful."

De Zavala's focus is on literacy and reading. Situated in East Houston, 92 percent of the school's students come from low-income households, and 98 percent are Latinx.[18] Many are learning English for the first time. To help get students excited about literacy and learning, the school participates in reading competitions. Along with rigorous coursework, these competitions have helped to significantly increase student academic achievement.

"Our students are competitive. We participated in a reading competition and we outperformed our competition by double the number of books read, because our students were really, really driven by that competitiveness in them," says Victoria Orozco-Martinez, the school's principal. "Because the reading had to be done at school, the students were asking 'Ms. Orozco, can we stay after school to read? Can we come on Saturdays to read?' So, we opened up after school and on Saturdays because of their competitive drive. Reading is a big component with every other subject."

Both of these schools offer advanced coursework, which is another trend in traditional public education that deserves more attention. According to the Education Commission of the States, nearly half of U.S. states now require traditional public schools to offer a specific amount of advanced coursework to students.[19] As a result, a record number of traditional public school students now take more rigorous math and science courses, according to data from the National Center for Education Statistics (NCES).[20] The College Board, which administers Advanced Placement exams, says that the number of high school students in public schools who take these exams increased by 65 percent over the past ten years.[21]

FOR MORE INFORMATION

To learn more about traditional public schools and open enrollment programs, you can visit the website of your local school district or state department of education. If you cannot easily find this information, please call your local school district or state department of education to ask for clarification. You can also visit the website for this book at schoolchoiceroadmap.com.

QUICK FACTS—TRADITIONAL PUBLIC SCHOOLS

Management/Governance

Traditional public schools are run by local school districts. School districts are usually overseen by elected school boards. All traditional public schools must follow the education laws in their states.

Costs

Traditional public schools do not charge tuition or entrance fees. Costs for traditional public schools are paid by taxpayers in the form of local, state, and federal taxes.

Enrollment

Traditional public schools generally must accept any child who applies to attend. In some specific circumstances, schools may be able to require students to take entrance exams for acceptance to a selective school for the gifted and talented.

Testing

After they are enrolled, students in traditional public schools are usually required to take annual or occasional state tests or assessments. These tests vary by state. Some school districts and individual schools have their own assessments, as well.

Teacher Certification

For the most part, all or most teachers in traditional public schools must be certified or licensed by the state to teach. Each state has its own teacher certification or licensure policies.

Students with Special Needs
Traditional public schools are required to enroll, and provide specific services for, children with special needs.

Transportation
Most states require that traditional public schools offer transportation to and from the school. Although rare, some school districts do not provide transportation for all students, or they provide transportation for a fee. In states that allow parents to choose schools outside of their zones or districts, transportation policies vary.

SNAPSHOT—TRADITIONAL PUBLIC SCHOOLS AND OPEN ENROLLMENT

While parents in every state can send their children to traditional public schools, each state has its own policies regarding open enrollment. Some states require school districts to let parents choose any traditional public school *within* their school districts. Other states require school districts to allow students to enroll in *any* traditional public school regardless of where they live. Meanwhile, some states let school districts decide if they want to participate in open enrollment programs. This table provides information on the open enrollment policies in each state. It is current as of July 2019. Updates and additional state details are available at schoolchoiceroadmap.com.

State	Does state law require school districts to let parents choose any traditional public school within their school district?	Does the state require school districts to let parents choose any traditional public school in any school district?
Alabama	No	No
Alaska	Yes, with limitations	No
Arizona	Yes	Yes
Arkansas	No	Yes, with limitations
California	Yes, with limitations	Yes, with limitations
Colorado	Yes	Yes
Connecticut	No	Yes, with limitations
Delaware	Yes	Yes
District of Columbia	Yes	DC has only one district
Florida	Yes	Yes
Georgia	Yes, with limitations	Districts can decide

Hawaii	No	State only has one district
Idaho	Yes, with limitations	Yes, with limitations
Illinois	Yes, with limitations	No
Indiana	Yes, with limitations	Yes, with limitations
Iowa	No	Yes, with limitations
Kansas	No	Districts can decide
Kentucky	Yes, with limitations	Districts can decide
Louisiana	Yes, with limitations	Yes, with limitations
Maine	No	Districts can decide
Maryland	No	No
Massachusetts	No	Districts can decide
Michigan	Yes, with limitations	Districts can decide
Minnesota	No	Yes
Mississippi	No	Yes, with limitations
Missouri	No	Yes, with limitations
Montana	No	Yes, with limitations
Nebraska	Yes, with limitations	Yes
Nevada	No	Districts can decide
New Hampshire	No	Districts can decide
New Jersey	No	Districts can decide
New Mexico	Yes, with limitations	Yes, with limitations
New York	No	Districts can decide
North Carolina	No	No
North Dakota	No	Districts can decide
Ohio	Yes, with limitations	Yes, with limitations
Oklahoma	No	Yes, with limitations
Oregon	No	Districts can decide
Pennsylvania	No	Districts can decide
Rhode Island	No	Districts can decide
South Carolina	N	Districts can decide
South Dakota	Yes	Yes

Tennessee	No	Districts can decide
Texas	Yes, with limitations	Districts can decide
Utah	Yes	Yes
Vermont	Yes, with limitations	Yes, with limitations
Virginia	No	No
Washington	Yes	Districts can decide
West Virginia	No	Districts can decide
Wisconsin	No	Yes
Wyoming	No	Districts can decide

Inspiration—A Profile of Burbank Middle School in Houston Texas

Atmosphere, accountability, and achievement are not just themes at Burbank Middle School in Houston, Texas. These terms define this traditional public middle school, which serves 1,500 students on the north side of Houston.

Regularly recognized as one of the best public middle schools in Houston, Burbank also performs better than 75 percent of middle schools throughout Texas.[22] At Burbank, 99 percent of students are either Latinx or African American, and more than 50 percent of students are current or former English language learners.[23] Almost every student comes from a low-income family and qualifies for free or reduced-price lunches.[24]

What are the keys to Burbank's success? Principal David Knittle gives the lion's share of credit to the school's teachers and their approach toward students. "We have a lot of systems in place that keep our campus running smoothly," he explains. "Our highly dedicated staff members and teachers put kids first before anything else...because student achievement is our number one focus. We want to provide a high-quality education for our students so that they're successful."

For Knittle, this means implementing a challenging curriculum called the Excel program that includes pre-AP courses for all students. It also means creating and expanding an effective gifted-and-talented magnet program called Vanguard. And it means offering a unique dual language program that allows some students to leave Burbank with not only a middle school diploma but also a certificate from a prestigious school in Spain.

Regardless of whether students pursue the Excel program, the Vanguard gifted and talented magnet program, or the dual language program, the school sets very high expectations. "It's rigorous instruction, and we also give kids extra time-on-task. We do after school work and tutorials on Saturdays, and we make sure we have high quality teachers teaching every subject," Knittle says.

Given that Knittle credits teachers with helping the school outperform its peers, finding great teachers and then rewarding and retaining them is understandably one of his top priorities. "When we interview people, we tell them, 'These are the expectations,' because it's a lot of hard work," he says. "In order for us to achieve the way we do, you have to do extra. There's no way around it."

That is why atmosphere, accountability, and achievement are goals for not only students but also for teachers and staff. Knittle says that adults at Burbank pay attention to every component that could impact student learning and teacher happiness. "We want to create an atmosphere of respect and trust for our students, a positive atmosphere not just emotionally, but physically," he says. "I like to keep the building as clean and orderly as possible."

He and his staff also focus on building extracurricular activities that are interesting and challenging so that the school does not become "so test focused" and impede student curiosity. "We have theater, we have choir, we have band, we have a Kickstart karate program that has been highly successful, with students winning top awards for everything," Knittle says. "Last year, I created an International Cultural Studies course, where students have the opportunity to study any kind of language that they want and do investigations and projects in regard to the language they learn. We also have a Hispanic American studies class. We have ballet, folklore, twirlers, and a huge cheerleading team."

chapter 4

PUBLIC CHARTER SCHOOLS

THE BASICS

Parents in forty-five states and the District of Columbia can choose to send their children to public charter schools.[25] These schools are managed by organizations, which receive permission to open charter schools from groups or agencies called charter school *authorizers*. Charter schools charge no tuition to attend and are always recognized as public sector, not private, schools.

There are more than 7,000 public charter schools across the U.S.[26] Charter schools must accept all students, regardless of their academic performance or needs. Students are not required to take special entrance tests for enrollment in a public charter school.

What makes public charter schools different from traditional public schools? Each public charter school focuses on a unique instructional method or strategy. This gives teachers and administrators the flexibility to try, or to replicate, innovative approaches to education. Public charter schools also have more freedom to develop their own curricula and practices.

YOUR CHOICES

Public charter schools were originally designed to be schools of choice. No student is ever automatically assigned to attend a public charter school. Instead, parents must select that school for their children. While some states have a wide variety of public charter schools in most geographic areas, other states place caps on the number of charter schools that are allowed to operate in the state.

In part because of these caps and limits, and also because of high demand among families, many charter schools have wait lists. If you enroll your child in a public charter school and he or she is not immediately accepted because the school is at capacity, the school is usually required to hold a random lottery to determine which students are admitted to the school.

My Take: Charter schools can transform ideas into realities

The entire concept of public charter schools is inspirational, because every charter school starts with an idea. Someone—often a teacher or former teacher—has the idea to create a new school focused on a specific instructional method or strategy. Perhaps the teacher thinks that students would benefit from more experiential, hands-on learning. Or, perhaps he or she thinks there needs to be a school that uses technology more effectively.

With that idea, the teacher—or a group of teachers, individuals, and community leaders—starts an organization. The goal of that organization is to open a new, tuition-free public school that is open to all students who apply. Once the school receives approval to operate, seeing the school open its doors for the first time is like watching an idea come to life.

The Howard University Middle School of Mathematics and Science in Washington, DC, provides a unique example of a fascinating idea coming to life as a public charter school. The school was created by Howard University educators as a way to build a pipeline so that students could ultimately consider careers in STEM. It is the only public charter school in the U.S. that is located on the campus of a historically black college or university (HBCU).

"Research shows that students actually figure out what they want to do from a career standpoint, believe it or not, at the middle school age," says Katherine Procope, the school's principal. "The university provides support by allowing our students to actually interact with professors here. We have students go to the university's chemistry department and do experiments."

In Vero Beach, Florida, Indian River Charter High School brought an educational idea to life, but with a different approach. Indian River focuses on character development, academic achievement, career preparation, and cultural awareness. The school was created and authorized by the Indian River County Public School District.

"We are a very family-oriented environment and we live by a code of mutual respect," explains the school's director, Cynthia

Trevino-Aversa. "Kids are here because they want to be here. We work together beautifully, and I believe that is what has made us successful. Our kids know us by name, we know them by name, we live our lives together on a daily basis in harmony, and we have created some unbelievable experiences and opportunities within these small walls."

At yet another public charter school, the idea that inspired the school's creation was to make college more attainable and affordable for students. At Baker Early College in Oregon, students not only graduate with a high school diploma; they also receive an associate's degree. This is because that public charter school, which focuses on accelerated learning, is partnered with fourteen community colleges and one university throughout the state to enroll students in college courses.

"The whole point of early college is if a student is ready to go to college while they're in high school, we want to facilitate and make that happen," explains Dan Huld, the school's superintendent. "In Oregon, one of the reasons that a charter school exists is to experiment with an idea—some kind of unique approach that's not available currently—and then take that idea, experiment with it and share back."

FOR MORE INFORMATION

To learn more about public charter schools, you can visit the website of the National Alliance for Public Charter Schools at publiccharters.org. The National Alliance is the nation's largest organization representing public charter schools and provides research, resources, and links to state-based charter school associations. Most of these state associations provide school finder maps and forms, allowing you to search for public charter schools in your area. The Center for Education Reform's website at edreform.com, also provides information about charter schools, as well as a tool that allows you to search for charter schools in your area. In addition, you can visit the website for this book at schoolchoiceroadmap.com.

Management/Governance

Public charter schools are operated by organizations. The vast majority of these organizations are set up as nonprofits.[27] Charter school authorizers oversee these organizations and make sure they are meeting the goals in the school's charter. Each state sets different rules on who can serve as a charter school authorizer. Some states require that school districts or state charter school boards serve as authorizers, while others allow universities or specific authorizing boards to serve this role. Public charter schools are required to follow state education laws and policies.

Costs

Public charter schools do not charge tuition or entrance fees. Most costs for public charter schools are paid by taxpayers in the form of local, state, and federal taxes. If you choose a charter school, there is nothing special that you need to do when you file your state or federal taxes; school districts and states allocate funds to public charter schools.

Enrollment

Public charter schools must accept any child who applies to attend. If there are more applicants to a school than available seats, a charter school is required to hold a random lottery to decide which students get to attend.

Testing

After they are enrolled, students in public charter schools are usually required to take annual or occasional state tests or assessments. These tests vary by state. Some school districts and individual schools have their own assessments, as well.

Teacher Certification

For the most part, all or most teachers in public charter schools must be certified or licensed by the state to teach. Each state has its own teacher certification or licensure policies.

Special Needs

Public charter schools are required to enroll, and provide specific services for, children with special needs.

Transportation

In about half of the states with public charter schools, charter schools are required to provide free and reasonable transportation to and from the school.[28] Other states do not require a specific type of transportation but require that charter schools develop transportation plans for their students. Some states do not have transportation requirements. Charter schools in these states sometimes offer their own transportation programs.

Most states allow for the creation of public charter schools. However, in some states, charter school options are limited to only a few schools throughout the state. This table provides information on the policies in each state. It is current as of July 2019. Updates and additional state details are available at schoolchoiceroadmap.com.

State	Does state law allow for the creation of public charter schools?	Are public charter schools available to families at least in some parts of the state, or is availability limited to only a few schools statewide?
Alabama	Yes	Limited
Alaska	Yes	Yes
Arizona	Yes	Yes
Arkansas	Yes	Yes
California	Yes	Yes
Colorado	Yes	Yes
Connecticut	Yes	Yes
Delaware	Yes	Yes
District of Columbia	Yes	Yes
Florida	Yes	Yes
Georgia	Yes	Yes
Hawaii	Yes	Yes
Idaho	Yes	Yes
Illinois	Yes	Yes
Indiana	Yes	Yes
Iowa	Yes	Limited
Kansas	Yes	Yes
Kentucky	Yes	Limited

Louisiana	Yes	Yes
Maine	Yes	Yes
Maryland	Yes	Yes
Massachusetts	Yes	Yes
Michigan	Yes	Yes
Minnesota	Yes	Yes
Mississippi	Yes	Limited
Missouri	Yes	Yes
Montana	No	N/A
Nebraska	No	N/A
Nevada	Yes	Yes
New Hampshire	Yes	Yes
New Jersey	Yes	Yes
New Mexico	Yes	Yes
New York	Yes	Yes
North Carolina	Yes	Yes
North Dakota	No	N/A
Ohio	Yes	Yes
Oklahoma	Yes	Yes
Oregon	Yes	Yes
Pennsylvania	Yes	Yes
Rhode Island	Yes	Yes
South Carolina	Yes	Yes
South Dakota	No	N/A
Tennessee	Yes	Yes
Texas	Yes	Yes
Utah	Yes	Yes
Vermont	No	N/A
Virginia	Yes	Limited
Washington	Yes	Limited
West Virginia	Yes	Limited
Wisconsin	Yes	Yes
Wyoming	Yes	Limited

Inspiration—A Profile of Cologne Academy in Cologne, Minnesota

As the spring weather gets warmer and summer break nears, teachers at Cologne Academy in Cologne, Minnesota do not count down the days until the school closes for the summer. The reason: too many students do not want school to end. They say they will miss learning, their teachers and their friends. That is because at Cologne, a public charter school serving children in grades K-8, learning is an adventure, one that is led by talented teachers who make it a point to build a school community in which people care about each other and share common values.

"With our school, you get a lot of value that can't be measured on standardized tests," says Lynn Peterson, the school's executive director. "I think you get a feeling of belonging. We know every student by name. There's a culture of accountability and responsibility, which is huge."

Peterson prefers not to discuss test scores, but this is not because the school is underachieving. Far from it. The school's aggregate scores in math, reading, and science are between 12 and 16 percentage points higher than average scores in the state.[29] Nearly three-quarters of Cologne Academy students take Algebra 1 before high school. To Peterson, though, these scores only tell part of her school's story. She is focused on making sure every child learns, including students who struggle.

"We are very intentional about telling students that they come here to learn, and that learning is their job," she explains. "'Your parents have their jobs to do, and learning is your work,' we tell them. Work sometimes can be hard. It sometimes can be frustrating…but every child needs success every day."

A key to maximizing school success is using a specific curriculum that focuses on literacy. Called Core Knowledge, this curriculum begins with "exposing students to a rich vocabulary, in kindergarten," Peterson says. "Even though they can't read some of these words, they can talk about the concepts. We want students to be literate and have a foundation in math, science, and history. Even if kids don't necessarily have a passion for, say, music, it is a core subject at Cologne Academy because it creates that shared literacy for a student going out into the world later on."

Beyond academics, Peterson says, "Part of our mission as a charter school is to strive to build students of character." That includes "explicitly teaching about a core virtue each month." Through student-teacher conversations on topics like respect and responsibility, honesty and integrity, generosity, gratitude, courage, loyalty, compassion, forgiveness, and diligence, students discover how these traits are important for learning, for life, and for their overall happiness.

Through all of the work that Cologne Academy does—whether in academics, sharing virtues, or through a variety of unique clubs and activities—Peterson wants teachers and school staff to demonstrate care for students. "I am passionate about what we do here, and I think that a key to our success is we have a good family here," Peterson says. "We work hard at positivity."

chapter 5

PUBLIC MAGNET SCHOOLS

THE BASICS

Parents in forty-six states and the District of Columbia can choose public magnet schools for their children.[30] These schools are managed by school districts, governed by local school boards, and charge no tuition to attend. In some cases, several school districts will work together as a group to create a public magnet school. Public magnet schools are always recognized as public sector, not private, schools.

There are more than 4,300 public magnet schools across the U.S.[31] At about 25 percent of public magnet schools, students must demonstrate academic qualifications or take entrance exams before being admitted to the school.[32] Three quarters of public magnet schools, however, have no entrance exams or academic requirements.[33]

Public magnet schools focus on specific themes, such as math, science, technology, the arts, or writing. However, public magnet schools are also required to teach all academic subjects. They use their themes as a way to get students excited about learning.

YOUR CHOICES

Public magnet schools were originally designed to increase diversity and inclusion within public school districts. Today, diversity remains a key focus of public magnet schools, as does theme-based learning. By their design, public magnet schools are schools of choice—meaning that children are rarely, if ever, automatically assigned by a district to attend a public magnet school. Instead, parents must select that school for their child.

While some states have a wide variety of public magnet schools, other states have fewer of these schools. Due to the popularity of magnet schools, many magnet schools have wait lists. Sometimes, school districts hold random lotteries to fill seats at magnet schools that are close to reaching capacity.

My Take: Magnet schools can combine
excitement with high expectations

When you walk into a public magnet school, you might immediately think to yourself, "Wow, there is something really cool about this place." During a tour of magnet schools in

Jacksonville, Florida five years ago, I had several of those "wow" moments. Kirby-Smith Middle School focuses on science, technology, engineering, art, and mathematics (STEAM). Just steps from the school's lobby is the Challenger Learning Center, a full space shuttle control room donated by NASA. The excitement at the Darnell Cookman Middle and High School in Jacksonville starts in the lobby as well. Visitors are greeted by students and teachers wearing medical lab coats, as this magnet school focuses on medical arts.

Magnet schools make learning exciting. That is by design. "A magnet school offers a specific program that is not generally offered in a traditional school," explains Joe Childers, the principal of Simon G. Atkins Academic and Technology High School in Winston Salem, North Carolina.

At Atkins—which requires no tests for entry—students can often be found programming video and computer games. But before they start coding, they are required to write handbooks about the games they are making. Childers says that this requirement helps students "to understand why it is important to write concisely." As a result, students at the school generally excel in English, in addition to science and math.

In nearby South Carolina, the Academic Magnet High School in Charleston sets high academic standards for entrance and also achieves stellar results. In fact, *U.S. News and World Report* recently named it the best public high school in America.[34]

"The idea behind Academic Magnet is to set a maximum, not a minimum, bar for a high school diploma," explains Catherine Spencer, the school's leader. Spencer says that the 162 students who graduated from the school in 2018 received an aggregate $14 million in college scholarships. The school's rigor, however, does not mean that it is not a fun and exciting place for students.

"We are very cognizant of the need for balance and the need to just breathe and have a good time and enjoy the comradery of our fellow students and staff members. That's a really integral part of what makes us a real community," Spencer says. The school's activities include competitive athletics, picnics, bubble soccer games, Powder Puff football, theme-based homecomings, and hallway decorating.

The excitement of public magnet schools is not limited to high schoolers. The New Emerson School at Columbus in Grand Junction, Colorado serves elementary and middle school grades. This unique school focuses on encouraging student learning through hands-on activities related to the STEAM curriculum. Recently, students and teachers at the school teamed with engineers to build a unique classroom called a *libratory*, which is a combination of a laboratory and a library.

Terry Schmalz founded the New Emerson School at Columbus. She is enthusiastic in her belief that having students "make things" helps them develop a passion for learning. "We believe that students need to be able to problem-solve and be creative and innovative," she says. "Those are some of the skills that they're going to need after they leave us, and so going through that whole 'making process'—the design process, the engineering process, working collaboratively, possibly with a partner or with a team—really does build those skills."

FOR MORE INFORMATION

To learn more about public magnet schools, you can visit the Magnet Schools of America website at magnet.edu. Magnet

Schools of America is the nation's largest membership organization for public magnet schools and provides a variety of
information about different approaches to magnet education.
To learn about magnet options near you, you can also visit the
websites of your local school district or state department of
education. Additional information is available on this book's
website at schoolchoiceroadmap.com.

Management/Governance
Public magnet schools are run by individual school districts or groups of school districts working together. All public magnet schools must follow the education laws in their states.

Costs
Public magnet schools do not charge tuition or entrance fees. Costs for public magnet schools are paid by taxpayers in the form of local, state, and federal taxes. If you choose a magnet school, there is nothing special that you need to do when you file your state or federal taxes; school districts and states allocate funds to public magnet schools.

Enrollment
According to Magnet Schools of America, 75 percent of public magnet schools do not require entrance examinations for students.[35] However, some schools are selective and set academic requirements for admission, including entrance exams.

Testing
After they are enrolled, students in public magnet schools are required to take annual or occasional state tests or assessments. These tests vary by state. Some school districts and individual schools have their own assessments, as well.

Teacher Certification

For the most part, all or most teachers in public magnet schools must be certified or licensed by the state to teach. Each state has its own teacher certification or licensure policies.

Special Needs

Public magnet schools are required to enroll, and provide specific services for, children with special needs.

Transportation

Public magnet school transportation policies vary by state and school district. Generally speaking, most magnet schools offer free transportation to students, although some do not.

SNAPSHOT—PUBLIC MAGNET SCHOOLS

All states allow for the creation of public magnet schools. However, in some states, there are no magnet schools in operation, or magnet school options are limited to only a few schools throughout the state. This table provides information on magnet school availability in each state. It is current as of July 2019. Updates and additional state details are available at schoolchoiceroadmap.com.

State	Does the state offer public magnet schools?	Are public magnet schools available to families at least in some parts of the state, or is availability limited to only a few schools statewide?
Alabama	Yes	Yes
Alaska	Yes	Yes
Arizona	Yes	Limited
Arkansas	Yes	Yes
California	Yes	Yes
Colorado	Yes	Yes
Connecticut	Yes	Yes
Delaware	Yes	Limited
District of Columbia	Yes	Limited
Florida	Yes	Yes
Georgia	Yes	Yes
Hawaii	No	N/A
Idaho	Yes	Limited
Illinois	Yes	Yes
Indiana	Yes	Yes
Iowa	Yes	Limited
Kansas	Yes	Yes
Kentucky	Yes	Yes

Louisiana	Yes	Yes
Maine	Yes	Limited
Maryland	Yes	Yes
Massachusetts	Yes	Yes
Michigan	Yes	Yes
Minnesota	Yes	Yes
Mississippi	Yes	Limited
Missouri	Yes	Yes
Montana	Yes	Limited
Nebraska	Yes	Yes
Nevada	Yes	Yes
New Hampshire	Yes	Yes
New Jersey	Yes	Limited
New Mexico	Yes	Limited
New York	Yes	Yes
North Carolina	Yes	Yes
North Dakota	No	N/A
Ohio	Yes	Yes
Oklahoma	Yes	Limited
Oregon	Yes	Yes
Pennsylvania	Yes	Yes
Rhode Island	Yes	Limited
South Carolina	Yes	Yes
South Dakota	No	N/A
Tennessee	Yes	Yes
Texas	Yes	Yes
Utah	Yes	Yes
Vermont	Yes	Limited
Virginia	Yes	Yes
Washington	Yes	Limited
West Virginia	Yes	Limited
Wisconsin	Yes	Limited
Wyoming	No	N/A

Inspiration—A Profile of Spring Hill High School in Chapin, South Carolina

Spring Hill High School in Chapin, South Carolina has a nearly perfect high school graduation rate and was recently named one of the best schools in South Carolina by *U.S. News and World Report*.[36] This public magnet school does not require any admissions tests for students to enroll. Instead, it relies on five core themes to engage students in their learning: engineering, entertainment, entrepreneurship, environmental studies, and exercise science.

At Spring Hill, students also learn all of their core subjects, including math, science, and history. According to the school's founder and principal, Dr. Michael Lofton, the school's five themes play a key role in accelerating learning across all subject areas. For example, if students in a class are interested in entrepreneurship, subjects are taught through that lens.

"As a class works through a math unit, a teacher at Spring Hill will embed a project-based learning activity that relates to that class of students' interests," Lofton describes. "That helps to hook the students into the math component. They really tend to delve a little bit deeper into study if they enjoy it more and it's something that they want to relate to."

Spring Hill High School's core classes and electives also benefit from access to the nearby Advanced Career and Technical Center, where students can learn more about anything from biological medicine to welding. "We make learning relevant to the kids' interests, and then the rigor comes after that," Lofton says. "Once you form connections and you make it interesting to those kids, they will go as far as you can push them."

Lofton, who was named the National Magnet School Principal of the Year in 2018, says that in addition to a rigorous and focused curriculum, the school's headline-making success is also attributable to the school's values.[37] "Our teachers are very approachable and spend a lot of time with students," he says. "We have one lunch period where our students are off for about fifty-five minutes in the middle of the day. You'll find teachers and students together during lunch studying, talking, and working on projects. We follow our little motto here. We call it the Spring Hill WAY, and the WAY stands for *working* with others, being *academically* focused, and *youth* inspired."

Lofton says that school choice works not only for students, but for his school's staff as well. That contributes to the school's enormous success. "When we talk about choice, not only do our students choose to come here, but all of my faculty, all of my staff, custodians, cafeteria employees...they also interviewed and wanted to be a part of this school as well," he says. "Everyone in this school community chooses to be at Spring Hill."

Lofton says that some people underestimate the hard work that goes into making sure students at his magnet school succeed. "We have no academic requirements to get into Spring Hill. It's a purely random, computer-generated lottery. We take 200 students per grade level. We have everything from Advanced Placement all the way to special needs co-taught classes here. It takes all of us—the entire school, parents, the community—heading in the same direction. If you put in that hard work and you're all moving in sync together in one direction, you're going to get great results."

chapter 6

ONLINE PUBLIC SCHOOLS

THE BASICS

Parents in thirty-two states and the District of Columbia can choose to send their children to full-time, online public schools.[38] Depending on the state, these schools can be managed by organizations, states, charter schools, or school districts. Online public schools charge no tuition to attend, and they are always recognized as public sector, not private, schools.

There are more than 300,000 students attending online public schools, on a full-time basis, across the U.S.[39] Online public schools must accept all students, regardless of their academic performance or needs. Students are not required to take special entrance tests for enrollment in online public schools.

Online public schools require students to use a computer, which is often provided by the school at no cost, to pursue their coursework. Students interact with real teachers using the internet, web cameras, telephones, and email. One hallmark of online public schooling is flexibility; students can often move through courses at their own pace, depending on their skills and needs. In many cases, parents and students are also able to set their own school day schedule. This allows students and parents to customize their learning schedule around the family's other obligations.

YOUR CHOICES

Online public schools are designed to be schools of choice. No student is ever automatically assigned to an online public school. Instead, parents must select that school for their child. In states with online public schools, there is usually availability. However, some states place caps on attendance or funding for these schools.

For students in elementary grades, online public schooling requires regular parent supervision and involvement. Middle and high school students may be able to pursue their learning without as much real-time parent supervision, depending on the child's needs. In some states, online public schools offer in-person service centers that students can visit to pursue some of their coursework or to meet with teachers or counselors.

My Take: Online public schools can harness
technology to empower flexible learning

If you hand many children an electronic device or a gaming system, they seem to instinctively know how to use it. This mastery of technology means that young people today have the ability to acquire knowledge at a faster rate than at any other time in human history. With online public schooling, students receive an education that is delivered using the devices they know and love. At the same time, they are learning in an environment that combines flexibility and rigor.

"Families enroll at our school for many different reasons," says Chris McBride of Nevada Connections Academy, an online public school. "Many families enjoy the flexibility that online school provides. There are specific tasks that need to be completed in certain timeframes, but families can get those done in a way that works for their schedule."

This flexibility means that online schooling meets the needs of many students who have busy schedules outside of their classrooms. For example, four figure skaters who represented the U.S. at the 2018 Olympics in PyeongChang attended California Connections Academy, an online public school.[40]

But online schooling is not just for students with athletic goals. There is a variety of reasons why families might find online education appealing.

"For every student, all 2,100 plus students of mine, there are 2,100 stories," says Suzanne Sloane, who runs the Virginia Virtual Academy, a K12 school. "Every single one of them has a different story about why they wanted to come here, but they really need this choice. I want people to know that students who have special needs and students who are gifted, they can all benefit.

"Some students enroll at our school because they are escaping some of the bullying issues that are present in brick-and-mortar schools," McBride says. "Other families enroll because they view it as an excellent alternative to homeschooling."

Those were just some of the reasons that Glenda, a mother from Buna, Texas, chose online public schooling for her daughter. "My child is thriving in online school. She is no longer crying every morning and evening. She is on a personalized learning plan. She's gifted in language arts, science, and any subject that requires reading. Her attitude is so much better with the flexibility and being able to learn other things in her spare time. She spends half the day working on other subjects that are not even offered for her grade level."

Just because online public schools are adaptable does not mean their curricula are easy. "Families can rest assured that they are getting a high-quality education and a college preparatory experience at Nevada Connections Academy," McBride says. "We have to be sure that they understand that online school here is not necessarily easier than brick-and-mortar schools."

According to Sloane, students who attend online public schools also have significant opportunities to meet and interact with other children. "One of the myths of virtual learning is that student don't get a chance to socialize," she says. "Our families will tell you that it is the polar opposite. Because they have the ability to be flexible with their scheduling, they actually have more opportunities to be with other students."

FOR MORE INFORMATION

To learn more about online public schools, you can visit the website of the National Coalition for Public School Options at publicschooloptions.org and that of the Digital Learning Collaborative at digitallearningcollab.com. These sites provide more information about online public school options in each state. You can also visit the website for this book at schoolchoiceroadmap.com.

QUICK FACTS—ONLINE PUBLIC SCHOOLS

Management/Governance

Online public schools are run by individual school districts, groups of school districts, state entities, organizations, or charter schools. All online public schools must follow the education laws in their states.

Costs

Online public schools do not charge tuition or entrance fees. Costs for online public schools are paid by taxpayers in the form of local, state, and federal taxes. If you choose an online public school, there is nothing special that you need to do when you file your state or federal taxes; school districts and states allocate funds to online public schools. In states without online public schools, tuition-based online private schools may be available.

Enrollment

Online public schools do not require entrance examinations for students.

Testing

After they are enrolled, students in online public schools are generally required to take annual or occasional state tests or assessments. These tests vary by state. Some school districts and individual schools have their own assessments as well.

Teacher Certification

For the most part, all or most teachers in online public schools must be certified or licensed by the state to teach. Each state has its own teacher certification or licensure policies.

Special Needs

Online public schools are required to enroll, and provide specific services for, children with special needs.

Equipment/Tech

In some states, online public schools are required to provide free computers and other technology to students. Some schools even cover internet access costs.

More than half of U.S. states allow for the creation of online public schools that enroll students on a full-time basis. In some states that do not have a full-time online schools, there are part-time, tuition-free, online public schools. This table provides information on online public school availability in each state. It is current as of July 2019. Updates and additional state details are available at schoolchoiceroadmap.com.

State	Does the state offer one or more full-time, tuition-free, online public schools?	If the state does not offer an online public school with full-time enrollment options, does the state offer a part-time, statewide, online school?
Alabama	Yes	–
Alaska	No	No
Arizona	Yes	–
Arkansas	Yes	–
California	Yes	–
Colorado	Yes	–
Connecticut	No	No
Delaware	No	No
District of Columbia	Yes	–
Florida	Yes	–
Georgia	Yes	–
Hawaii	No	Yes
Idaho	Yes	–
Illinois	No	Yes
Indiana	Yes	–
Iowa	Yes	–
Kansas	Yes	–
Kentucky	No	No

Louisiana	Yes	–
Maine	Yes	–
Maryland	No	No
Massachusetts	Yes	–
Michigan	Yes	–
Minnesota	Yes	–
Mississippi	No	Yes
Missouri	No	No
Montana	No	Yes
Nebraska	No	No
Nevada	Yes	–
New Hampshire	Yes	–
New Jersey	No	No
New Mexico	Yes	–
New York	No	No
North Carolina	Yes	–
North Dakota	No	Yes
Ohio	Yes	–
Oklahoma	Yes	–
Oregon	Yes	–
Pennsylvania	Yes	–
Rhode Island	No	No
South Carolina	Yes	–
South Dakota	No	No
Tennessee	Yes	–
Texas	Yes	–
Utah	Yes	–
Vermont	No	Yes
Virginia	Yes	–
Washington	Yes	–
West Virginia	No	Yes
Wisconsin	Yes	–
Wyoming	Yes	–

Inspiration—GOAL Academy in Colorado

Eighteen-year-old Max Emory is joining the Coast Guard when he graduates from high school. But his path to serving his country has not been an easy one. Max and his family moved twenty-three times over the course of his life. With all of that upheaval, Max worried that he wouldn't be able to succeed in high school. Then he found GOAL Academy.

GOAL Academy is an online public school serving more than four thousand students in Colorado. Students at GOAL primarily pursue their courses online. GOAL also offers twenty-eight drop-in centers throughout the state where students can meet with teachers, coaches, counselors, and even social workers.

"The ability to move around and keep going to the same school has really helped my education," Max says. "I haven't had a stable life, and this is something stable. This is something that I can work with, no matter what. Nothing about the school is going to change for me."

According to Constance Jones, GOAL Academy's chief executive officer, the school's approach is designed to meet the unique needs of students in different situations. The school provides each student with a free computer and internet hot spot so that there are "no barriers to allowing students to succeed."

"We call our school a blended model. Students are able to work online, but come in for tutoring and support," Jones says. "Our drop-in centers are open from 9 a.m. to 5 p.m., but depending on student needs and our populations in our different communities, we'll also offer evening hours and additional time. Our school runs the gamut of serving at-risk students, students with special learning needs, students who are gifted and talented, and students who want to learn at their own pace."

In addition to providing a high school education, the school offers college credit for some courses through a concurrent enrollment program. For students who want to pursue careers or trades, instead of heading to college, the school has the option to provide them with experience and work skills, too. Jones says that the school has a variety of apprenticeship programs, including "part-time jobs, full-time jobs, internships, apprenticeships—whatever we can work out—to maintain a focus on career and technical education."

These programs are all part of GOAL's efforts to address the individual interests, challenges, and, as you might expect, goals of each student. "Every student here can expect a personalized plan to ensure that they are taking the appropriate courses to help them finish their high school diploma," Jones says. "They can also count on a staff that is very caring—a staff that will stay right there with them the whole, entire way in supporting them, encouraging them, and checking in on them to make sure everything's okay."

GOAL student Max Emory offers some smart advice for families and students considering online public schools. "To be honest with you, you just have to put in the work," he says. "You can do it at home. You can do it on-site, anywhere with internet access. The teachers have everything set up in the proper format, and things are easy to understand. If you keep up with your work, and you don't fall behind, there's no stress."

chapter 7

PRIVATE SCHOOLS

THE BASICS

Parents in every community across the U.S. can send their children to private schools. These schools are managed by private or religious organizations, and they charge tuition to attend. While some states require private schools to be accredited, licensed, or approved, private school rules are mostly set by the schools themselves and not by any government entity.

There are more than 34,000 private schools across the U.S.[41] These include faith-based schools and independent schools. Private schools determine their own admissions policies, and some private schools set academic requirements or require entrance examinations for enrollment.

YOUR CHOICES

Private schools are always schools of choice in that no student is ever automatically assigned to attend a private school by any district or agency. Parents must select these schools for their children. In many cases, parents are able to consider a wide variety of private school options in their regions. However, other communities have fewer private school options.

Most private schools offer scholarship opportunities for students who excel academically or whose parents cannot afford tuition. Local nonprofit organizations also offer scholarships in many communities. In some cities and states, affiliates of Children's Scholarship Fund or ACE Scholarships—organizations that provide need-based K-12 private school scholarships—offer tuition assistance, too.

In twenty-nine states and the District of Columbia, state-sponsored programs have been established to help families afford the cost of tuition.[42] These programs vary significantly in their size and scope. Some programs cover the full cost of tuition for qualifying families, while others cover only a portion of these costs. These programs are referred to by several different names, including opportunity scholarships, tax credit scholarships, empowerment scholarships, school vouchers, education savings accounts, or tuition tax deductions.[43]

My Take: Private schools can be unique, diverse,
and more affordable than you might think

When you think of private schools, what comes to mind? If you attended private school yourself, you might have an idea of what to expect. But maybe you are envisioning an ornate old building covered in ivy, walled off from its neighbors, complete with an expensive tuition.

These elite, expensive, and secluded private schools do indeed exist, but they represent only a tiny fraction of the private schools across the country. Private schools in America are, by and large, diverse in every way. They include independent schools and schools that are centered around every possible religion and faith. Many private schools are affordable, and most offer scholarships. Private schools also play key roles in the communities they call home.

Cornerstone Preparatory Academy, a Christian school in Acworth, Georgia, provides an example of how a unique private school can provide affordable education options and improve its community at the same time.

Originally opened in 2004 by Jeanne and Fred Borders, the school serves 600 students across grades K-12. Cornerstone offers a university-style schedule and charges by the semester hour.

"This allows a less expensive private school tuition," explains Jeanne Borders, who adds that "close to one hundred students receive scholarship money" from Georgia's state-sponsored scholarship program.

In addition to rigorous academics, Cornerstone places a strong emphasis on community involvement. For example, students participate in a week of service activities instead of spring break. High school seniors must implement a service project as a requirement for graduation. Projects have included everything from blood drives to efforts to benefit foster children.

Service projects offer "a tremendous experience for students and creates a better environment," Borders says. "There is such excitement and energy."

The Learning Tree Cultural Preparatory Center in the Bronx provides another example of diversity, rigorous academics, and affordability within the private education sector. Learning Tree combines academic coursework with service-oriented international trips and in-school activities. "Our philosophy is that inner-city children should be able to experience anything that other children experience," explains Lois Gregory, the school's founder. "Also, we wanted to find something that could enrich all our students' lives. So, we developed a performing arts program: dance, drumming, visual arts, and music. It's a very vibrant part of our school."

Many of the students at Learning Tree receive scholarships from Children's Scholarship Fund, a national nonprofit organization that helps low-income families afford private school tuition.

The North Florida School of Special Education in Jacksonville, Florida provides another example of a trend in private education: the fact that many private schools are specifically designed to serve children with special learning needs. At the North Florida School, students learn in a dynamic environment that includes a berry orchard, a culinary program, and the support of a therapy dog named Zenbowie. Sally Hazelip, one of the founders and the current head of school at the North Florida

School, describes the school as "the happiest place on earth."

Florida's state-funded scholarship programs, which are among the most flexible and generous in the country, play key roles in making this unique school accessible to families. "I think our families are very thankful to our state government for the McKay and Gardiner scholarship programs," Hazelip says. "All of our kids receive some form of scholarship and it helps significantly with the tuition and gives families a chance that they otherwise might not have had."

FOR MORE INFORMATION

To learn more about private schools in general, you can visit the website of the Council for American Private Education (CAPE) at capenet.org. CAPE represents most of the private school organizations across the country and provides links to these organizations. To learn more about state-sponsored private school scholarship programs, the websites of EdChoice at edchoice.org and the American Federation for Children at federationforchildren.org are helpful. You can also visit the website for this book at schoolchoiceroadmap.com.

QUICK FACTS—PRIVATE SCHOOLS

Management/Governance

Private schools are operated by organizations and governed by boards of directors. Every state has different rules for private schools. Many states require private schools to be accredited, registered with the state, licensed by the state, or approved to operate in the state.[44] The majority of states regulate the minimum number of days students must be in school each year.[45] Private schools are also generally required to follow safety, health, and building codes. Some states also require private schools to teach specific courses. In most cases, these requirements mean that private schools must teach a certain number of classes in core subjects like math, science, and English.[46]

Costs

Private schools charge tuition. Some schools also charge application fees. Many private schools have scholarships available for students whose parents cannot afford tuition. Local, state, and national scholarship organizations also provide privately funded scholarships. In twenty-nine states and the District of Columbia, parents will find state-supported scholarship programs that help families cover all or part of private school tuition.[47] Sometimes, these programs are run and administered by the state. In other cases, they are managed by private organizations, such as Step Up for Students in Florida. These state-supported scholarships are usually limited to students from low- or middle-income families or families with special needs children. The scholarships are often referred to as opportunity scholarships, scholarship tax credits, special needs scholarships, education savings accounts, or school vouchers. Some states also provide state tax deductions or credits for parents who send their children to private schools.

Enrollment
Every private school sets its own enrollment policies.

Testing
Students in private schools are generally not required to take state education tests. However, many schools have their own standardized tests. Some states with state-funded scholarship or tuition assistance programs require students who receive scholarships to take state standardized tests.

Teacher Certification
Private schools generally set their own rules for hiring teachers. Some schools participate in certification or licensure programs. Sometimes, these programs are run by private organizations rather than the government.

Special Needs
Many private schools offer services to students with special learning needs. Some private schools are specifically designed to help students with learning needs. Other private schools may not have the capability to serve students with certain learning needs.

Transportation
Private school transportation options vary by school.

SNAPSHOT—PRIVATE SCHOOL TUITION ASSISTANCE PROGRAMS

Parents in all U.S. states can send their children to private schools. More than half of U.S. states offer some type of state-sponsored private school scholarship or tuition assistance program for families. Some states also allow parents who send their children to private schools to receive income tax credits or deductions to help offset the cost of private school tuition. This table provides information on state-sponsored private school choice program availability in each state. It is current as of July 2019. Updates and additional state details are available at schoolchoiceroadmap.com.

State	Does the state sponsor programs that allow qualifying students to receive scholarships or private school tuition assistance?	Does the state allow eligible parents to deduct all or a portion of private school tuition from their state income taxes, or receive a tax credit for tuition?
Alabama	Yes	Yes
Alaska	No	State doesn't have an income tax
Arizona	Yes	No
Arkansas	Yes	No
California	No	No
Colorado	No	No
Connecticut	No	No
Delaware	No	No
District of Columbia	Yes	No
Florida	Yes	State doesn't have an income tax

Georgia	Yes	No
Hawaii	No	No
Idaho	No	No
Illinois	Yes	Yes
Indiana	Yes	Yes
Iowa	Yes	Yes
Kansas	Yes	No
Kentucky	No	No
Louisiana	Yes	Yes
Maine	Yes	No
Maryland	Yes	No
Massachusetts	No	No
Michigan	No	No
Minnesota	No	Yes
Mississippi	Yes	No
Missouri	No	No
Montana	Yes	No
Nebraska	No	No
Nevada	Yes	State doesn't have an income tax
New Hampshire	Yes	State doesn't have an income tax
New Jersey	No	No
New Mexico	No	No
New York	No	No
North Carolina	Yes	No
North Dakota	No	No
Ohio	Yes	No
Oklahoma	Yes	No
Oregon	No	No
Pennsylvania	Yes	No
Rhode Island	Yes	No

South Carolina	Yes	Yes
South Dakota	Yes	State doesn't have an income tax
Tennessee	Yes	State doesn't have an income tax
Texas	No	State doesn't have an income tax
Utah	Yes	No
Vermont	Yes	No
Virginia	Yes	No
Washington	No	State doesn't have an income tax
West Virginia	No	No
Wisconsin	Yes	Yes
Wyoming	No	State doesn't have an income tax

Inspiration—A Profile of Plato Academy in Des Plaines, Illinois

How can a school build a culture of respect? For the leaders of Plato Academy in Des Plaines, Illinois, it starts with giving students a voice in how they learn. If students at this private, independent, K-8 school seem particularly interested in a topic, teachers work with them to keep exploring that subject in class and through activities. Plato Academy's principal, Marianthi Koritsaris, describes it as an "authentic curriculum."

For example, when students expressed interest in the Notre Dame cathedral fire in Paris on April 15, 2019, they started studying French landmarks, worked to learn about the potential impact of robotics on the cathedral's restoration, and learned how to build models of the cathedral and other buildings to scale. "So, they're studying social studies, literature, they're writing about things, their reading is emerging from this, and they are learning math concepts," Koritsaris explains.

Part of encouraging students to pursue these interests and develop a respect for learning is to foster open dialogue. Students at Plato Academy do not need to raise their hands to get recognized by a teacher. "This way, kids can't hide in the back and not raise their hand, because everybody is part of all conversations, and equally involved with the teacher," Koritsaris says.

Students are also encouraged to talk with their parents about their schooling. Plato Academy teachers do not assign traditional homework, such as worksheets or quizzes. Instead, families are asked to read together.

The culture of respect at Plato Academy does not just extend to a respect for learning. Students discover the importance of respecting their community. Instead of mandating that students pursue community service projects, Plato Academy students are encouraged to find ways to give back to their communities in their own ways. Recently, a group of young students pursued a project to help raise awareness about clean drinking water. Another group of students worked to provide stuffed animals to children whose homes had burned down.

Students also discover the importance of respecting each other. The school has a strong nondiscrimination statement, which is part of an effort to make everyone feel welcomed at Plato Academy. "If we're going to prepare kids for the real world, you can't pick and choose who you're going to work with, who is going to be living in your neighborhood with you," Koritsaris says. "I think that kids need to form communities with a diverse group of people, so we find that community building is really rooted in making memories together."

The result is a school in which students feel valued and are motivated to learn. "Our students are more than ready for high school, and not only the academic challenge of high school, where most of them end up in honors and Advanced Placement classes," says Koritsaris. "They also distinguish themselves in their high schools in a variety of ways, by joining the debate team, or going into sports and becoming the captains of their teams. They're not intimidated. They know they are capable. They walk in very boldly."

chapter 8

HOMESCHOOLING

THE BASICS

Parents in every community across the U.S. have the freedom to homeschool their children. Homeschooling rules and policies vary between states. For example, some states require that homeschoolers provide a one-time or annual notice to the state or to a local school district. This notice indicates that the family intends to homeschool their children. In other states, no notice is required at all.[48]

Beyond just notice requirements, states also have different approaches to regulating homeschooling. Some states require homeschool families to teach specific subjects, and others require homeschoolers to take annual standardized tests. Other states have none of these requirements.[49]

Opportunities for homeschooling students within the public education system also vary. In more than half of U.S. states, homeschoolers have the right to access some public sector school sports, interscholastic activities, or public school classes.[50] Other states prohibit homeschool students from participating in these activities.[51]

YOUR CHOICES

Homeschooling requires a commitment of time and effort. In exchange for that dedication, homeschoolers have the flexibility to design their own curricula, set their own school schedules, and pursue their own educational interests.

There are more homeschool support groups, networks, and collaboratives than ever before to help homeschool families navigate the process. In addition, there are online resources, classes, and curricula that parents can use to augment their own instruction. Homeschool families can also work together to hire private tutors or teachers for certain subjects so that students can learn together. These are just some of the reasons that homeschooling continues to grow by approximately 2 percent per year, with more than 2.3 million U.S. students currently educated in the home.[52]

My Take: Homeschooling can offer customized
learning and exploration, on your terms

Homeschooling is often described as the *original school choice*. In reality, homeschooling was the only choice for a portion of our country's history. That is because, for many families in the past, there were no public schools for children to attend. Before the mid-1800s, most education took place in the home, by private tutors, or at private or common schools. Fourteen U.S. presidents and four U.S. Supreme Court justices were homeschooled.[53]

Today, homeschooling is incredibly diverse. According to a review of homeschooling research in the *Journal of School Choice*, "It is clear that parents who identify as liberal, progressive, conservative, and libertarian are all involved in homeschooling. Multiple studies indicate that home education is common among agnostics, atheists, Christians, Jews, Mormons, New Age adherents, and Roman Catholics." The study also indicated that homeschooling was geographically widespread, with "62 percent of homeschool students [living] in cities and suburban areas, while the others live in towns and rural areas."[54]

Homeschooling is popular because it provides a pathway to a completely customized educational experience for children. This experience means that millions of different students from different backgrounds are learning in millions of different ways.

Tonya, a mother in Concord, North Carolina, says homeschooling is important for her children because she can "choose curricula and teaching methods that foster learning, understanding and application. We can move faster or slower or right on pace, depending on interest, understanding, and ability."

She explains that homeschooling allows her to turn everyday situations into learning opportunities. "We literally 'learn' everywhere we go and in everything we do," she says. "Because I am the teacher, I know exactly what and when our students were introduced to a subject or topic."

For Anita in Jackson, New Jersey, the choice to homeschool her children has allowed her kids to be themselves. "School choice for my family is what gives us personal understanding of how to work on your strengths, and without feeling obligated to be what others want you to be. You can also work on your weaknesses without pressure from anyone. My children are not judged by only their abilities, but they are encouraged to think for themselves, too."

Parents who homeschool their children tell me that the process requires dedication and commitment. But it does not always require moms and dads to adjust their work schedules to accommodate a normal school day schedule. Homeschooling, instead, often allows for maximum flexibility.

Flexibility is exactly why Lindsay, a mom in Overland Park, Kansas, chose homeschooling. It meant reducing the number of interruptions in her child's educational experiences. "Our family has relocated many times due to my husband accepting job promotions," she says. "Homeschooling has allowed us to transition to new destinations without gaps or overlaps in curricula. With so many changes that come with relocating, at least schoolwork and routines are able to remain stable and our family can flourish together."

For most homeschooling families, positive family life is rivaled only by the results of the education they have provided their children. "We decided that homeschooling was best. Ten years later, we have graduated two children and one is finishing up," says Jodi, a mom from Indian Trail, North Carolina. "You have to be brave in your choice. Not everyone will support your choice, no matter what it is. Know your 'why' and be okay with other people's choices."

FOR MORE INFORMATION

To learn more about homeschooling, you can visit the website of Home School Legal Defense Association (HSLDA) at hslda. org. HSLDA provides thorough information about home-schooling laws across the country and provides links to state and local homeschooling organizations. Most states offer a variety of homeschool organizations, networks, and support groups. Additional information is available from the National Home Education Research Institute at nheri.org. You can also visit the website for this book at schoolchoiceroadmap.com.

QUICK FACTS—HOMESCHOOLING

Management/Governance

Homeschooling families are responsible for their own children's education. States set their own requirements for homeschooling families, often requiring notices of intent that families must submit to homeschool their children. Some states also require that homeschool parents teach their children specific subjects.

Costs

All costs for homeschooling are paid for by homeschooling families themselves. Parents do not receive any federal tax relief for choosing to homeschool their children, although some states offer state tax deductions and allowances for instructional materials and educational expenses.

Enrollment

Parents who choose to homeschool their children usually must formally unenroll their children from the schools they previously attended. Most states also require parents to inform, or provide notice to, their home school district or to the state if they intend to homeschool their children. Sometimes, this notice must take place on an annual basis. In other states, only a one-time notice is required.[55]

Testing

Less than half of U.S. states require some level of assessment, either annually or periodically, of homeschool students.[56]

Parental Requirements

In less than half of U.S. states, parents must meet specific criteria or qualifications, such as requiring a parent to hold a high school diploma, to homeschool their children.[57]

Access to Programs

In more than half of U.S. states, homeschooled children are generally allowed to participate in extracurricular, interscholastic, or athletic programs offered within the public school system.[58] Some states also allow parents to enroll homeschooled children in specific classes at local public schools or online public schools, as well. These policies often provide for some limitations or exceptions. For example, some states allow homeschooled students to participate in activities but only at the discretion of local public school district officials.

Parents in every U.S. state have the freedom to homeschool their children. Each state sets its own homeschooling policies and regulations. This table provides information on homeschool notice and sports participation policies in each state. It is current as of July 2019. Updates and additional state details are available at schoolchoiceroadmap.com.

State	Does the state require parents to provide notice, on either a one-time or annual basis, that they intend to home-school their children?	Does the state require school districts to allow homeschooled students to participate in public school sports and activities?
Alabama	Yes	Yes
Alaska	No	Yes, with limitations
Arizona	Yes	Yes
Arkansas	Yes	Yes, with limitations
California	Yes	No
Colorado	Yes	Yes
Connecticut	No	No
Delaware	Yes	No
District of Columbia	Yes	No
Florida	Yes	Yes
Georgia	Yes	No
Hawaii	Yes	No
Idaho	No	Yes, with limitations
Illinois	No	Yes, with limitations
Indiana	No	Yes, with limitations
Iowa	No	Yes, with limitations
Kansas	Yes	No
Kentucky	Yes	No

Louisiana	Yes	No
Maine	Yes	Yes, with limitations
Maryland	Yes	No
Massachusetts	Yes	Yes, with limitations
Michigan	No	No
Minnesota	Yes	Yes, with limitations
Mississippi	Yes	No
Missouri	No	No
Montana	Yes	No
Nebraska	Yes	Yes, with limitations
Nevada	Yes	Yes
New Hampshire	Yes	Yes
New Jersey	No	Yes, with limitations
New Mexico	Yes	Yes, with limitations
New York	Yes	No
North Carolina	Yes	No
North Dakota	Yes	Yes, with limitations
Ohio	Yes	Yes
Oklahoma	No	No
Oregon	Yes	Yes
Pennsylvania	Yes	Yes
Rhode Island	Yes	Yes, with limitations
South Carolina	Yes	Yes
South Dakota	Yes	Yes, with limitations
Tennessee	Yes	Yes
Texas	No	No
Utah	Yes	Yes
Vermont	Yes	Yes, with limitations
Virginia	Yes	Yes, with limitations
Washington	Yes	Yes, with limitations
West Virginia	Yes	No
Wisconsin	Yes	Yes, with limitations
Wyoming	Yes	Yes

Inspiration—A Profile of RISE Homeschooling Resource Center in Las Vegas, Nevada

Elissa Wahl did not expect a summer day at Long Beach Island to shape her son Brian's educational future. She simply wanted to show him a local lighthouse and then head to the beach to enjoy the sun and water. Brian had different plans. He simply could not get enough information about that lighthouse.

"There was a plaque outside of the lighthouse that said, 'The first lighthouse was washed into the ocean. This is a re-creation,'" Elissa Wahl describes. "Brian was three years old and wanted to know what the original lighthouse looked like. He wouldn't stop asking, and nobody could tell us the answer."

So, Elissa and Brian visited the local historical society. Then, they headed to the library. Then, they talked to some elderly residents in the community. Brian never got an answer, but Elissa knew at that point that her son loved to learn. "What that day showed me is that it's very important to take into consideration my son and his interests in his own learning," she says. That day also convinced Elissa to homeschool Brian.

Elissa designed a unique curriculum for her son that focused on, you guessed it, lighthouses. They traveled up and down the East Coast, visiting lighthouses and learning. "It was an incredible education that I was able to provide him all based on one specific interest that he had," she says. "So, we learned geography, history, ocean life, marine sciences, all sorts of things."

A New Jersey resident at the time that she started homeschooling, Elissa moved to Nevada in 2000. She soon discovered that the state's homeschooling requirements were more restrictive and that state lawmakers were considering legislation that would have required homeschooling parents to use specific textbooks instead of being able to customize their own curricula. That law would have made Elissa and Brian's lighthouse journey all but impossible.

Even though she was new to the state, Elissa worked with other homeschool parents to pass a more flexible set of state policies for homeschooling. Her experience as a homeschool mom led her to want to help other homeschooling families in Nevada navigate the homeschooling process. So, she created the RISE Homeschool Resource Center, a nonprofit organization headquartered in Las Vegas.

RISE frequently gets calls from parents who really want to homeschool their children but are plagued by a crisis of confidence. "The most common thing parents say is, 'How can I homeschool if I don't even understand my kids' homework?'" Wahl describes. "I explain to them that this is not a good comparison. You don't know your kids' homework because you're not in the classroom. You don't know how the teacher's teaching it. You don't have the teacher manual." Wahl reminds families that if they homeschool, they get to select their own curricula.

Wahl also wants parents to know that "the first year of homeschooling is the roughest."

"Because most of us have come from a traditional school background and we think we have to mimic public school at home. [But] homeschooling does not need to look like public school. You need to figure out what's going to work for your family. If you want to do math and reading on Monday, and art and science on Tuesday, that's totally up to you."

chapter 9

UNIQUE APPROACHES
TO EDUCATION

AS YOU PURSUE THE SCHOOL SEARCH PROCESS, you might research a school and ask, "What type of school is this?" and receive an answer that does not fall neatly into one of the six types of schools you just read about. That is because some schools describe themselves based on the *services* they offer, a specific instructional *strategy* that they use, or their educational *philosophy*. In some cases, you will find schools of different types that share similar approaches to education.

CHOICES WITHIN CHOICES

Here are several examples of different descriptions and classifications that schools use to describe the work that they do, and the different ways that these schools can be managed and run:

- **Alternative** schools are primarily for students with disciplinary or behavioral issues. However, with the growth of school choice options, schools with different approaches have started positioning themselves as *alternatives* to traditional learning environments. These schools exist across all types of schools, and all types of schools can have alternative education programs.

- **Arts** schools focus on one or more artistic disciplines, such as performing arts, communication arts, drama, and music. These schools exist across all types of schools, and all types of schools can have arts programs.

- **Boarding** schools allow students to live in school-based housing, similar to a college or university. While boarding schools are usually private schools, there are also some boarding schools that have been established as public charter schools. In the future, we might even see boarding schools organized as public magnet schools as well.

- **Career and Technical** schools prepare students "for the world of work by introducing them to workplace competencies, [making] academic content accessible to students by providing it in a hands-on context."[59] Students at these schools are generally provided with an education that prepares them to go either to college or directly into the workforce. These schools exist across all types of schools, and all types of schools can have career and technical programs.

- **Dropout Prevention and Recovery** schools are designed for students who have dropped out of school, need to make up credits, or are at risk of leaving school. These schools exist across all types of schools, and all types of schools can offer dropout prevention and recovery programs.
- **Gifted and Talented** schools are for students who have specific academic or artistic talents. A school that specifically and solely admits students who are gifted and talented could be organized as a selective traditional public school, a public magnet school, or a private school. Within all types of schools, you are likely to find gifted and talented education programs.
- **International Baccalaureate (IB)** schools are authorized by the IB Organization as IB World Schools. These schools "aim to do more than other curricula by developing inquiring, knowledgeable and caring young people who are motivated to succeed."[60] All types of schools are eligible to be authorized by the IB organization.
- **Laboratory** schools are affiliated with colleges and universities and work to prepare teachers and students under the guidance of recognized college scholars or "master teachers."[61] These schools exist across all types of schools.
- **Language Immersion** schools teach children multiple languages. At these schools, students and teachers frequently speak in foreign languages as part of their daily curricula. These schools often combine "two language education models: an immersion program for English-only speakers and a bilingual maintenance model for English learners."[62] These schools exist across all types of schools, and all types of schools can use language immersion programs.

- **Military** schools provide a structured atmosphere and prepare students for careers in service to our country. These schools aim to "provide students with the skills, confidence, and resilience necessary to guarantee their success in whatever career they pursue."[63] While most military schools are private, they can exist across all types of schools. In addition, many schools offer Junior Reserve Officers' Training Corps (JROTC) programs, even if they do not classify themselves as military schools.

- **Montessori** schools adhere to the instructional strategy developed by Dr. Maria Montessori. This strategy "is student-led and self-paced but guided, assessed, and enriched by knowledgeable and caring teachers, the leadership of their peers, and a nurturing environment."[64] These schools exist across all types of schools, and all types of schools can use a Montessori approach to teaching.

- **Progressive** schools focus on an educational approach known as progressive education. These schools aim to "nurture citizens in an increasingly diverse democracy" by fostering solidarity and dialogue between students, teachers, and communities and promoting "diversity, equity, and justice in our schools and society."[65] These schools exist across all types of schools.

- **Semester** schools offer an approach to education that allows students to travel and experience other cultures, explore specific interests, or pursue a customized curriculum for a specific length of time. These are usually private schools, but students from all types of schools can qualify to attend a semester school.

- **Single-Gender** schools admit either only boys or only girls. These are usually private schools. However, there are examples of single gender schools of all types of schools.

- **Special Needs** schools provide specialized education to students with disabilities or special learning needs. Some of these schools serve students with a wide range of intellectual differences, while others focus on students who have hearing or vision impairments, autism, or dyslexia. These schools exist across all types of schools.
- **STEM** schools focus on science, technology, engineering, and math. These schools exist across all types of schools, and all types of schools can have STEM programs.
- **Vocational** schools offer "a sequence of courses which are directly related to the preparation of individuals in paid or unpaid employment in current or emerging occupations requiring other than a baccalaureate or advanced degree."[66] These schools exist across all types of schools, and all types of schools can have vocational programs. These schools are often similar to career and technical schools.
- **Waldorf** schools adhere to an instructional strategy developed by a scientist named Rudolph Steiner. These schools "integrate the arts in all academic disciplines for children from preschool through twelfth grade to enhance and enrich learning."[67] These schools are usually private schools or public charter schools, but other types of schools can also use a Waldorf approach or program.

Families considering homeschooling will find a variety of different instructional methods and approaches that they can use. There are resources and curricula available that reflect almost all of the different descriptions and classifications we have discussed.

There is one type of educational approach that is restricted to private schools and homeschooling families: religious education.

There are private schools and homeschooling programs that are centered around almost every possible religious congregation and faith. With that said, not all private schools are religious and not all homeschooling resources are faith-based. There are thousands of non-sectarian independent schools across America, and many of them embrace some of the approaches and methods we have just discussed. Traditional public schools, public charter schools, public magnet schools, and online public schools are never permitted to focus on one religion.

MOVING FORWARD AND NEXT STEPS

Every child is unique, and every child deserves an education that is inspiring, motivating, and challenging. As a parent, you want your son or daughter to succeed in school and in life. You also want your child to pursue happiness and achieve his or her dreams. Across our country, amazing teachers and community leaders have created so many different types of schools. The landscape of education in the U.S. is truly remarkable, with more variety and diversity than at any other time in history.

Now, it is time for you to start the process of deciding which school or learning environment will meet your child's needs. That is the fun part! But before you proceed to Part Two of this book, let's take a moment to recap Part One:

- School choice is an extension of the choices we make every day. It is a process of identifying what you need and want for your child, and then considering your options. School choice options have grown to meet our nation's demands, and many parents have more choices for their children's education today than ever before.

- Choosing a school or learning environment for your child can increase your child's chances at finding success and happiness. Parents who actively choose schools for their children are more satisfied with the education their children receive than parents who have no choices or do not actively choose schools or learning environments.
- School choice doesn't just help individual students and families; it helps communities. Having different types of schools can help bring greater education diversity and variety to a community.
- As your child's parent, you know your child best. Education can sometimes appear confusing and filled with jargon, but your intuition and understanding of your child's needs is the most important factor in the school search process. You are your child's greatest advocate and cheerleader. You are the expert.

In Part Two, you will put this knowledge—as well as the information you gathered about the six different types of schools—into action. Most importantly, you will take what you know about your own educational experiences, your child's needs and interests, and what you need and want in a school to design your own roadmap to choosing a school or learning environment that meets your child's needs. Onward!

> *"Sometimes changing schools can be frightening, even for parents. And it does come with its own struggles. But you overcome them together. It not only makes you stronger as a family but playing a larger role in my children's education gives me pride."*
>
> JILL, A MOTHER FROM MONESSEN, PENNSYLVANIA

"I wouldn't just go off of others' opinions on their choices. Each child is their own person and will learn their own way. Give your gut a chance and see for yourself."

DANA, A MOTHER FROM LANSING, MICHIGAN

"School choice has meant that I am able to give my teens with high anxiety the freedom to carve out their own learning path as they grow and figure out their way in life while still knowing that my younger kids have the foundation and help they need."

SHIRLEY, A MOTHER FROM MEMPHIS, TENNESSEE

Quick Takes: Unique approaches, interesting perspectives

Discover some of the perspectives, strategies, and educational techniques that are helping to make education in America diverse and unique. Just as every child is unique, every school is, too.

* * *

U.S. News and World Report recently named **Dr. TJ Owens Gilroy Early College Academy** in Gilroy, California one of the best high schools in America and the third best high school in California.[68] Sonia Flores, the principal at this traditional public school, describes Gilroy's early college model.

> "An early college is a program that allows students to be dually enrolled, and it's a partnership between, in most cases, a community college and a K-12 school district. The students are placed at this special type of program where they take high school classes for part of the day, and they also take college classes for part of the day. Those college classes that they take count towards both their high school diploma, but they also count towards an AA degree or a four-year university degree. Just this year, 74 percent of the graduating class petitioned for their AA degree, and participated in the graduation ceremony."

At **Providence Hebrew Day School** in Providence, Rhode Island, students from all faiths learn together. At the high school level, the school offers a boarding school model that brings students from across the Northeastern U.S. and even from around the world. Rabbi Peretz Scheinerman, the dean of the school, talks about the importance of inclusion in private education.

> "We have students from across the religious Jewish spectrum, and some students whose parents may not be Jewish. We're not a school that looks to missionize people to become more religious. We're a school where kids learn by example, and where kids make choices in life based on the examples that they've witnessed and seen. Kids are very involved here. There are no 'upperclassmen' in this school, so twelfth graders respect ninth graders, and ninth graders respect twelfth graders, and boarders respect local kids, and local kids respect boarders. It's mutual acceptance across the board."

* * *

Michigan Connections Academy is a full-time, online public school serving students across Michigan. Bryan Klochack, the school's principal, talks about the process of educating young students via online coursework.

"We work within a self-contained environment. The courses and the lessons are available to the kids twenty-four hours a day, seven days a week. Flexibility is important because certainly, we don't expect a kindergarten or young elementary student to be on the computer for seven hours a day. That's not good practice. So, the importance of the role of what we call the Learning Coach—which is an adult at home with the student—is helping make sure students stay on task. We don't ask them to be the instructors, but at home they do play a service. And a lot of times, parents come to us because they want to have a more active role in their child's education. We're pleased with that because at the base of our program is the relationship between the teacher, the student, and the parent."

* * *

Morning Star School in Jacksonville, Florida recently celebrated its first-ever high school graduation. This Catholic school focuses on providing a tailored education for children with special learning needs. Principal Jean Barnes talks about how Morning Star School works to combine a unique educational setting with activities that students enjoy.

"One of the most beautiful things about our high school is we know that academically, we were going to be the best place for these kids, but we wanted to find a way to make sure they had that rich, full high school experience. We have partnered with Bishop Snyder High School, and our kids attend all their dances, they attend prom and homecoming, attend all the pep rallies, and they go to retreat days. They have peer mentors at Snyder. They are able to participate in that full, big high school experience, socially and spiritually, while getting the academics they need here."

* * *

Brethren Christian School in Riverside, California recently made headlines after students convinced NASA to install one of the school's science experiments onto the International Space Station. Dr. John Moran, the principal of this private school, credits parent mentors with inspiring students to pursue the project, and discusses the importance of mentorship in Christian education.

"I believe that in education, we are mentoring in everything and helping students to make a positive impact on society. So, mentors are key [for programs like] our service trips and mission trips. In Honduras, we have mentors leading a team of our students to go to Montagna de Luis, an orphanage where all the orphans have HIV. We do building projects and other service projects and spend time with the children. Christian schools…should go out and interact with the world and serve the world. Jesus gave us the example of service and we should follow that but try to give the students as many practical ways to do that as possible."

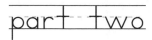

part two

SEVEN STEPS TO CHOOSING A SCHOOL OR LEARNING ENVIRONMENT FOR YOUR CHILD

overview

AT THIS POINT, you have read about school choice in general, the importance of finding a school or learning environment that meets your child's needs, and the different types of schools that may be available.

Remember, none of the information you have read so far is more important than what you know about your own child. You are the expert, and your expertise and intuition will guide you through the next part of this book—the seven steps to choosing a school or learning environment for your child.

These steps are based on my conversations with, and

feedback from, thousands of parents and school leaders. They focus on choosing the right school or learning environment for *your child*, not finding a school that *other people* might think will be effective. What works for most students, many students, or even some students, might not be effective for your son or daughter.

The seven steps provide a practical plan for putting your knowledge, values, and goals into action. Here is an overview:

Step 1: Think back to your own time in school

In this step, you will look back at your own experiences in school. You will examine what you loved the most, learned the most, and liked the least, about your own educational experiences. Sure, it might sound strange right now, but this exercise will prove helpful. This will help you put your own values, views, concerns, and expectations down on paper and place the entire school search process into a more personal context.

Step 2: Identify your goals for your child

Your big goal in reading this book is to find a school that meets the needs of your child. But in Step Two, you won't be thinking about schools just yet. Instead, you will *tell your story* and write down your own hopes, dreams, and goals for your child—specifically as they relate to your child's learning and development.

Step 3: Decide what you need and want from a school or learning environment

In Step Three, you will think about the things that matter most to you in a school or learning environment. You will identify your top priorities and specific priorities. You will also fill out a Priorities Worksheet that will play a key role as you pursue the next steps in this process.

Step 4: Make a list and research schools

Step Four might be time consuming, but it's important. To choose the right school or learning environment for your child, you need to know what options are available. In this step, you will research school choice policies in your state and make three lists of schools. You will start with a big list, and, through the different techniques in this step, you will narrow down your options.

Step 5: Visit schools

In this step, you will discover everything you have ever wanted to know—and possibly some things you didn't—about school tours. School tours are important, and this step provides a comprehensive guide. We will cover everything, including how to schedule a school tour, to what to look for while you are walking through a school, and what questions you should consider asking.

Step 6: Evaluate schools

This step will help you narrow down your list of schools once again. If, after your research and school tours, you have already identified a few schools or learning environments that you love, this step will be easy for you. But if you can't make up your mind, you will find several evaluation techniques and suggestions that you can use. Your goal will be to narrow your school search down to two or three finalists from which to choose.

Step 7: Choose the school or learning environment that meets your child's needs

Once you get to Step Seven, you have reached the end of the school search journey! In this step, you will discover tips on applying to schools, work through the process of making your final decision, and learn more about different ways that you can prepare your child to succeed in his or her new school or learning environment.

WHEN SHOULD YOU START?

When should you start this process? Right now! If you want to find a new school or learning environment for your child, there is no wrong time to start searching. However, there are times that may be more advantageous for you. I recommend starting this process in the winter—so that you can enroll your child in a school, or pursue homeschooling, for the next school year. One of the reasons that we celebrate National School Choice Week in January is so that parents can use the week to start this process, visit schools, consider their options, and still have time to make a decision with enough lead time.

Some parents are surprised when I recommend starting this process in the winter, because they think it might be too early. In reality, it's not. Starting in the winter gives you the opportunity to pursue these steps without rushing. It also increases your chances of finding schools that have availability. Schools that are popular among parents tend to reach capacity—meaning they cannot enroll any more students because they are out of space—more quickly. Even though you might not end up choosing a popular school, you will not want to limit your options.

However, some families do not have the luxury of time. You

might be starting this process in the late spring, or you might need to make a quick change or a fast choice. In those cases, I encourage you to accelerate the first few steps in this process so that you can schedule your school tours quickly—especially before schools close for summer break.

HOW TO PURSUE THE SEVEN STEPS

As you read through these steps, please keep an open mind and pace yourself. These steps cannot be completed in a single day. While you might be able to complete the first few steps in a short amount of time, your school research, school tours, and school evaluation and decision process will take longer.

Ideally, you should start by completing Steps One through Three. These steps focus on self-evaluations and setting priorities. Then, start working on Step Four—researching school choice policies and making lists of schools. Finally, complete the process with Steps Five through Seven, which entail visiting schools, evaluating them, and making your final decision.

You might consider reading through all of the steps before you embark on the process, so that you can get an idea of what to expect. If you choose to do that, remember that choosing a school or learning environment is indeed a *process.* And remember: nothing about this process is designed to steer you toward, or away from, one type of school or learning environment. If you have any questions about school choice, you can flip to the Frequently Asked Questions section at the end of Part Two, at any time.

One final note: in some cases, you will notice that online public schools and homeschooling are specifically mentioned. These mentions are not designed to prioritize or discourage these options. Looking at online public schools and homeschooling, in addition to all other options, is important to a well-rounded school search process. But because these environments do not have physical school buildings, you will find several different ways to make sure that they are fully considered.

With that said, are you ready? Let's go!

Important: this section includes a variety of worksheets, surveys, exercises, and forms. I encourage you to write your answers directly in the book. Alternatively, you can download full-sized, printable versions of these forms online at schoolchoiceroadmap.com.

step 1

THINK BACK TO YOUR
OWN TIME IN SCHOOL

THINK BACK to your experiences in school. Think about the teachers who made a difference in your life, the most important things you learned, the skills you discovered that you now use every day, the classes that inspired you, and the clubs and activities that helped you discover your interests. This is not just a theoretical question. Take a moment to think back. Can you remember a moment when a teacher or club advisor said something to you that literally changed the trajectory of your learning, and your life? Or, did you have an experience that was so upsetting that you can recall it like it happened yesterday?

Okay, I will go first. My first in-school "change your life" moment was in the first grade. Everyone in class was taking turns standing up and reading out loud from the book, *Have You Seen My Duckling?*, as part of a class exercise. When it came to my turn to read, I froze. *There is no way I can do this*, I thought. *I'm too scared*. Even though my mother and father read to me every night, I was nervous about reading in front of the class.

My teacher, Mrs. Jarnecki, called my name. I didn't move from my seat. "OK, it's your turn," she said. "Come on up and speak, Andrew."

"I really don't want to," I whispered to her. "I don't think I can do it."

She looked at me calmly and walked over to my desk. She leaned down, put her hand on my arm, and said, "Trust me. You can do it, Andrew. Just try."

I got out of my seat and walked slowly to the front of the room. I started reading from the book. Almost instantly, I realized that not only could I read and speak at the same time, I loved doing it. The intimidation, fear, nervousness, and self-doubt melted away.

To this day, I love reading and writing. As for public speaking, I regularly give speeches to groups of hundreds and sometimes thousands of people. I always prepare for these engagements, but I am rarely nervous. When I think back to elementary school, I wonder what path my life would have taken if Mrs. Jarnecki had not encouraged me to stand and read out loud, or what might have happened if my parents hadn't read to me each evening.

The way I view education and learning is shaped by this

experience. I tend to place a huge emphasis on reading. In some of my previous writing, I have referred to reading as the "cornerstone subject." But I also realize that someone could have had an amazing experience in math and might consider that subject to be even more valuable to them.

Now, it is your turn. Take your experiences and put them onto paper. Perhaps you had a very positive experience in school, like I did. Or, maybe you look back with regret that your school was not the right fit for you. Reflecting on these things can be helpful. Your own experiences *will* influence the school search process in ways that you might not realize right now. Use the question prompts on the Step One Worksheet to dig deep into your memory.

What was your most positive learning experience?

What subject or class in school has had the biggest impact on your life, and why?

What classes in school did you find most engaging or interesting, and why?

What three teachers had the biggest, most positive impact on your life?

_____

_____

_____

What were three of your accomplishments or achievements in school?

_____

_____

_____

What are your best overall memories from school?

Is there anything you wish you learned—but didn't—in school?

What school subjects did you find the most difficult?

What classes did you find least engaging or interesting, and why?

What are your worst overall memories from school?

What are your overall views on the quality of education in our country? In your state? In your community?

Do you still live in the community where you grew up? How do you think the schools you attended have changed over the years?

REVIEWING YOUR ANSWERS

It may have felt a bit strange, even invasive, to complete an assessment of your own educational experiences. After all, you are choosing a school for your child, not for yourself. However, as uncomfortable as it may have been, it serves an important purpose: to allow you to remember and acknowledge things from your own history that might impact the decisions you make for your child's education. The Step One Worksheet was designed to help you better understand why you have a "gut" reaction to certain types of learning environments, bringing greater context to your intuition as a parent.

As you move forward to Step Two, please reread your Step One Worksheet responses. Your educational experiences and memories are important, but you should also take into account that your child will not necessarily react the same way to specific environments, classes, instruction methods, and experiences that you did. It is also important to note, especially if you are considering sending your child to the same school you attended, that schools can change significantly over the years, for better or for worse.

step 2

IDENTIFY YOUR GOALS
FOR YOUR CHILD

WHETHER THEY'RE A CAB DRIVER, doctor, barber, attorney, or waitress, I talk to parents about their children's education almost every day. (The unluckiest people are those who are forced to sit next to me on a plane.)

As soon as someone asks me what I do for a living, I tell them I work in education. Then, I start asking them broad questions about their own experiences. As I mentioned in the introduction to this book, asking people to tell me their stories elicits more authentic answers than asking specific questions.

Almost every parent I meet talks about education in a way

that is interesting, relevant, and emotional. Parents tell me how their children's schools stack up to their own values and their own experiences. They talk to me about whether their children are learning. They tell me that their children are safe and are happy. They are excited that their children are succeeding. Or, they are worried for their children—worried that they are falling behind academically, are unsafe, regularly unhappy, or are struggling. In short, parents speak from the heart.

It does not matter if the parents I meet are wealthy or financially struggling; if they live in big cities or rural towns; or whether they work in professions, trades, factories, or retail. All parents frame their views on education, and their satisfaction or dissatisfaction with schools, through the lens of the all-encompassing values they personally hold dear and through their perceptions of their children's well-being.

Using the Step Two Worksheet, we are going to have a similar conversation. Obviously, we are not sitting face-to-face, but I want you to *tell me your story.* Use this worksheet to write down your hopes, dreams, and goals for your child. Think about your child's uniqueness and your family's values and principles.

After reading about school choice and the different types of schools in Part One—and assessing your own educational experiences in the Step One Worksheet—the Step Two Worksheet will help you to refocus your thinking by focusing on the single most important person in the school search process: your child.

If you could look into the future and think of one word to describe the type of person you want your child to be, what word would you choose? Fill in the blank.

I hope that my child will be: _____.

What are three words that best describe your child right now?

_____

_____

_____

What are three values, traits, or life lessons that matter most to you and your family—the things you hope your child will learn from you?

_____

_____

_____

What are the three most important *subjects* that you want your child to learn in school—meaning the three subjects that you believe will be most important for your child's future success?

_____

_____

_____

What are the three most important *skills or traits* that you want your child to learn at school and at home—meaning three broader things that are not necessarily related to specific subjects but that you think are important?

_____

_____

_____

What are three things that interest your child the most? These don't have to be academic subjects. They can be anything that sparks your child's curiosity!

_____

_____

_____

Describe the types of settings or environments where your child seems to best absorb or acquire knowledge and information. What do they look like?

Describe the types of settings or environments where your child is least likely to absorb or acquire knowledge and information. What do they look like?

What do you think are your child's greatest academic strengths?

What academic subjects do you think your child might struggle with the most?

Does your child have special learning needs that should be specifically addressed at school? What are those needs?

Has your child had previous experiences in a school or educational setting? If so, what were the things you liked the most about that setting, and what do you wish you could have changed?

Now, what were the things about that setting that you wish you could have changed the most?

Regardless of how you define "happiness," what are the three things, settings, or experiences that make your child happiest?

What are your three biggest worries or concerns for your child's future?

What about your child's learning needs is different from what you would have wanted for yourself in a school or learning environment?

Thinking of your child's learning and development, how do you define success? What does success look like for your child and for your family?

REVIEWING YOUR ANSWERS

The purpose of Step Two and the worksheet that you just completed is to refocus your thinking. Ultimately, this entire process is not about any one school or educational environment. A school will exist long after your child moves on or graduates. So, even though this process focuses on schools and learning environments, it is really about *your child*. By completing the Step Two Worksheet, you set the stage to think more about all of the things you need and want from a school for your child. This is helpful preparation for Step Three, in which you will get even more specific.

Before moving to Step Three, please reread your assessment answers once again. Did you write anything that surprised you? Did you write anything that caused you to think differently about what you need or want for your child and his or her learning? Please remember these things, as they will come in handy as you move forward in this process. Then, proceed to the next step.

step 3

DECIDE WHAT YOU NEED AND WANT FROM A SCHOOL OR LEARNING ENVIRONMENT

BY THIS POINT, you have explored your own educational experiences. Most importantly, you have also spent time thinking about your child and his or her needs. Please do not discard what you have written; you will need it later on when we talk about the role this information plays in your ultimate school choice.

In Step Three, you will specify the things that you need and want most in a school or learning environment for your child. You will first develop a list of *top priorities*—the things that you *need* from a school or learning environment. These are big, broad priorities; they are things that are absolutely essential to your ultimate decision. Then, you will develop a list of *specific priorities,* the things that you *want* a school or learning environment to focus on or offer for your child.

You will write your top priorities and specific priorities on a Priorities Worksheet, which is located on page 150. Your Priorities Worksheet will be important as you pursue the remaining steps in the school search process.

Before we dive into the details of Step Three, I encourage you to take a moment and clear your head. Close your eyes. Think about your child and imagine them learning in an environment where they are safe, happy, and successful. *What* would this environment offer? *Why* would it be perfect for your child? *How* would it be unique? Keep these things in mind, as this brief exercise will set the stage for you to develop a solid list of top priorities and specific priorities.

TOP PRIORITIES

First, think big. To start the process of determining your top priorities—the most important things that your child needs from a school or learning environment—I encourage you to complete the following statements: "My child needs a school or learning environment that…" and "I need to find a school or learning environment that…"

As you think about the way you would finish these statements, consider the big, broad values that are important to you and your family and the things that reflect your goals, dreams, and aspirations for your child.

To give you some food for thought, let me share with you some of the things that many parents have told me are their top priorities. The following commonly shared top priorities—which might seem like commonsense values in education and schooling—will help you to hone and refine your own list of top priorities, which you will list in the Top Priorities section of the Priorities Worksheet on page 150:

- *Learning*—It almost goes without saying, but parents tell me they that need schools in which their children will actually *learn*. They say that they need schools that set high expectations for their students, offer rigorous and relevant coursework, hire and retain knowledgeable and caring teachers, do everything possible to make sure that every child is learning at or above their grade level, and regularly monitor students' progress to make sure that no one is falling behind.

- *Safety*—Whether you drop your child off at a bus stop in the morning, take your child to school yourself, watch as your child logs in to an online course, or educate your child in your home, you never stop caring about your child's physical and emotional well-being. Parents and children need schools and learning environments in which students are safe and protected—schools with well-executed plans for preventing and addressing violence, drug use, fighting, and bullying.

- *Mutual respect*—Respect is an important value not only in education but in life. We all have our own definitions of respect, but parents often tell me that mutual respect is vital to them when searching for a school or learning environment for their child. For example, parents say that they need schools that respect students of all backgrounds and cultures, schools that respect diversity in their hiring practices, schools that respect a child's disabilities or intellectual differences, and schools in which parent input is respected and valued.

- *Happiness*—Parents know that few children will love every moment of every day in school. Setbacks and struggles are normal parts of life. But parents also know that when a child's school environment is the root cause of persistent unhappiness, that child's well-being is affected. Parents tell me that they need schools at which their children learn to set and achieve goals, build strong characters, build their confidence, and develop positive relationships with others—because all of these things can impact their happiness, learning, and development.

- *Success*—The four top priorities that we just discussed add up to something that sounds simple but is very powerful: parents need schools and learning environments in which their children will have every opportunity to succeed, both in school and in life. Parents need to know that the big dreams and aspirations that they have for their children can be realized, and the school or learning environment that they choose will help, not hinder, that progress.

Do you share these priorities? Do you have other needs or top priorities that are important to you and are specific to your family's situation? For example, if you are searching for a school or learning environment that aligns with your faith, values, or beliefs, that would be considered a top priority for you. Turn to the Priorities Worksheet on page 150 and fill in your answers.

SPECIFIC PRIORITIES

Now, let's get specific and explore what you want a school or learning environment to *offer* for your child. These are things like a school's academic offerings, instruction strategies, educational themes, curricula, climate, courses, activities, sports, services, or environment. To identify your specific priorities, I encourage you to complete the following statement: "I want to find a school or learning environment that offers…"

Truthfully, there are *hundreds* of factors that education researchers say might impact a student's achievement or success in school. You know your child best, and you are best equipped to decide which factors will have the biggest impact on your child's learning and success.

To give you some food for thought that will help you refine your specific priorities, we will once again look at some of the priorities that other parents frequently tell me are important to their children's success in school. I should note that most parents discuss only a handful of these priorities, not all of them. Using the Specific Priorities Rating Exercise, you can identify whether any of the specific priorities I describe are:

- A priority for you
- Neither important nor unimportant to you (neutral)
- Not a priority for you

These items are not listed in order of any perceived importance, and they are not grouped together in categories. They are, again, food for thought. So, be honest in your assessments and in how you rate each item. Once you are finished rating these items, you will identify your own specific priorities and finalize your Priorities Worksheet.

Read each of these possible priorities. Then, circle whether you consider each of these items to be:

- A priority for you
- Neither important nor unimportant to you (neutral)
- Not a priority for you

When you are finished, you will evaluate your ratings and continue adding to your Priorities Worksheet.

A focus on core subjects

Do you want a school that focuses specifically on core subjects, such as reading, writing, math, science, and history, so that your child can demonstrate mastery of these subjects? Some parents believe that an active focus on "the basics" will best prepare their children for life.

Yes—Priority   Neutral   No—Not a priority

Competency-based education

Do you want a school that focuses on teaching students skills rather than abstract theories? In the competency-based education approach, students learn one skill at a time. Once they master each skill, they move on to the next one.

Yes—Priority   Neutral   No—Not a priority

Critical thinking
Do you want a school that focuses on cultivating critical thinking skills in students? These skills include interpreting and analyzing problems and challenges, evaluating possible solutions to specific problems, communicating with others, and, ultimately, solving problems.

Yes—Priority   Neutral   No—Not a priority

Character development
Do you want a school that pays particular attention to building students' characters? This could include educating students on honesty, decision-making, trustworthiness, personal ethics, compassion, fairness, morality, and citizenship.

Yes—Priority   Neutral   No—Not a priority

A specific instructional strategy or methodology
Do you want a school that offers a specific instructional strategy such as cooperative learning, differentiated instruction, individualized instruction, direct instruction, or inquiry-based teaching? Some parents know which instruction methods work best for their children.

Yes—Priority   Neutral   No—Not a priority

Extra focus or emphasis on a specific subject

Do you want a school that focuses on a specific subject or theme, such as reading, foreign language immersion, English Language Learner (ELL) education, STEM, or gifted and talented education? Some parents know that their children need or benefit academically from a specific focus.

Yes—Priority   Neutral   No—Not a priority

Art and music programs

Do you want a school that prioritizes art and music education? Some students find greater learning—along with greater inspiration and happiness—through art and music classes, activities, or programs.

Yes—Priority   Neutral   No—Not a priority

Use of modern or advanced technology

Do you want to find a school or learning environment with a specific approach to using technology? Some parents know that their children acquire knowledge more quickly when they are paired with effective technology, while other parents find that technology distracts their children.

Yes—Priority   Neutral   No—Not a priority

Number of students in the school

Do you want a school that—in terms of the total number of students enrolled—is smaller or larger than most? Some students learn more in smaller schools that have fewer students, while other students find that they benefit from schools with more students.

Yes—Priority   Neutral   No—Not a priority

Student-to-teacher ratio or class size

Do you want a school that has a specific student-to-teacher ratio or class size? Some students might learn more effectively in smaller classes, while other students might feel more comfortable—and thus learn more effectively—in larger classes.

Yes—Priority   Neutral   No—Not a priority

A school that offers a career and technical education program

Do you want your child to learn about a trade, craft, or specific type of career while in school? These programs can include career-focused studies on everything from health care to technology, culinary arts, vehicle repair, plumbing and carpentry, and more.

Yes—Priority   Neutral   No—Not a priority

A school that offers advanced coursework or programs for gifted students

Do you want a school that offers a specific set of advanced coursework, such as honors courses, Advanced Placement (AP) classes, an International Baccalaureate (IB) curriculum, or a program designed to serve gifted and talented students?

Yes—Priority   Neutral   No—Not a priority

A school that offers catch-up courses or credit recovery programs

Do you want a school that provides opportunities for students who have struggled in specific subjects or previously failed classes to be able to retake these classes using a different instructional strategy that might be a better fit for them?

Yes—Priority   Neutral   No—Not a priority

A school that prioritizes social-emotional learning

Do you want a school that prioritizes social-emotional learning (a learning strategy that focuses on helping students work with teachers and parents to learn emotion management, how to set and achieve goals, and how to show empathy for others)?

Yes—Priority   Neutral   No—Not a priority

A variety of activities and sports programs

Do you want a school that offers sports programs, clubs, activities, and extracurriculars? Some parents seek schools that offer specific activities, while other parents simply want a variety of sports or activities from which their child could choose.

Yes—Priority   Neutral   No—Not a priority

A specific homework policy

Do you want a school that has a specific approach to or policy regarding student homework? Some parents feel that too much homework can have a negative effect on student learning. Other parents believe that if students receive no homework, they might miss out on learning opportunities.

Yes—Priority   Neutral   No—Not a priority

A specific approach to standardized testing or test prep

Do you want a school that offers a specific approach to standardized testing or preparation for standardized testing? Some parents find these assessments to be valuable tools, while other families worry that too much "test prep" takes away from learning.

Yes—Priority   Neutral   No—Not a priority

A school that embraces community service/involvement
Do you want a school that emphasizes community service, volunteerism, or community involvement? Some parents believe that their children's learning is positively affected by these types of programs and by increased community involvement in schools.

Yes—Priority   Neutral   No—Not a priority

A school's atmosphere or environment
Do you believe that your child's learning will be affected significantly by things like the cleanliness, noise, temperature, lighting, air quality, or accessibility of a school building? Do you have a particular atmosphere- or environment-related concern?

Yes—Priority   Neutral   No—Not a priority

A discipline policy that you agree with
Do you want a school that offers a specific approach to student discipline? For example, some parents might want a school with a stricter approach, while other parents prefer more leniency. Some parents feel that a specific discipline policy has a significant impact on their child's learning.

Yes—Priority   Neutral   No—Not a priority

A school that offers "wraparound" services, such as nutrition or after-school programs
Do you want a school that offers a breakfast program, an after-school care program, social services, counseling, or health services?

Yes—Priority   Neutral   No—Not a priority

NEXT STEPS

Hopefully, this exercise gave you the chance to think more deeply about what you want in a school or learning environment. Have you thought of any specific priorities that matter to you but were not listed on the Specific Priorities Rating Exercise? For example, some parents might consider the following to be specific priorities:

- Finding a school that does not charge tuition or offers a full scholarship
- Finding a school that has transportation to and from school
- Finding a school that is geographically close to your home

Now, turn to the Priorities Worksheet on page 150. Identify five specific priorities that are most important to you in a school or learning environment. These can be priorities from the Specific Priorities Rating Exercise or other priorities that you have identified. Write your answers on the worksheet. Once you have completed the Priorities Worksheet, you can proceed to Step 4.

Top Priorities

At the beginning of this step, I shared five top priorities that many parents say are essential in a school or learning environment. Do you agree? If so, check the box next to each item so that you can remember these priorities throughout the school search process.

I need to find a school or learning environment:

      ____ in which my child will learn
      ____ in which my child will be safe
      ____ that embraces the importance of mutual respect
      ____ that will maximize my child's happiness
      ____ in which my child will succeed

Now, identify two or three of your own top priorities. To help you do this, you can simply finish the following statement: "I *need* to find a school or learning environment that..." or "My child *needs* a school or learning environment that..."

_____

_____

_____

Specific Priorities

Now, identify five specific priorities. You can use the examples provided in the Specific Priorities Rating Exercise, or you can simply finish the following statement: "I *want* to find a school or learning environment that offers…"

_____

_____

_____

_____

_____

Once you have completed your Priorities Worksheet, you are ready to move on to Step 4. However, make sure to keep the Priorities Worksheet handy, as it will play an important role in the rest of this process.

step 4

MAKE A LIST AND
RESEARCH SCHOOLS

NOW THAT YOU HAVE IDENTIFIED your priorities, the fourth step in your school search process is to:

- Identify the different school choice programs and policies in your area
- Make a big list of schools in your area
- Narrow down that list
- Learn more about those schools
- Narrow your list down further

To complete this step, you will need access to the internet. Making lists, narrowing them down, researching the schools, and narrowing your list down further will also take some time. But this is an important part of the school search process. You do not want to accidentally overlook a school that might be a good fit just because you did not know it existed in the first place.

IDENTIFY THE SCHOOL CHOICE PROGRAMS AND POLICIES IN YOUR AREA

First, it will be helpful for you to discover some of the different school choice policies in your state or area. At this point, you are not looking for individual schools, but simply discovering what types of schools might be available and what level of access you will have to them. To do this, I recommend visiting this book's website at schoolchoiceroadmap.com. There, you will find information and links that will help you answer the following questions:

- Does your state allow parents to choose traditional public schools outside of your geographic boundary or zone? This is an important question to answer because if your state allows you to choose a school outside of your zone or district, you do not want to limit your search. You will want to find out, specifically, what options are available and what limitations or exclusions apply to choosing a traditional public school outside of your area.

- Does your state allow for the creation of public charter schools? If so, are charter schools widely available for families in your area? Some states allow for the creation of public charter schools, but have very few of these schools in operation, while other states have a large number of public charter schools available.

- Does your state have public magnet schools available? If so, are public magnet schools widely available for families in your area? While all states allow for the creation of magnet schools, some states do not have many of these schools in operation.
- Does your state have full-time, online public schools?
- Does your state have a state-supported private school choice program in addition to scholarships offered by individual schools and local organizations?
- What are the requirements that families must meet if they want to homeschool their children?

In addition to the reference materials in this book and online, families in some areas can find answers and support from local organizations that have been set up to help parents navigate the school search process. These organizations are often called "parent navigators." For example, parents who live in major metropolitan areas of California, Illinois, Louisiana, Massachusetts, New Jersey, Ohio, Tennessee, and Texas can access services from organizations that match parents with advisors—at no cost—and help them through the school search process. Other nonprofit organizations, social service agencies, or religious organizations provide similar services in different communities.

MAKE YOUR FIRST LIST (A.K.A. THE "BIG LIST")

After you have finished evaluating the programs and policies in your area, it is time to make a big list of schools and learning environments to consider for your child's education. To start, you will need to decide how far away you are willing to send your child to school, whether the distance is just a few miles, a few dozen miles, or in your home. This will help you set some basic parameters so that your list is not too small or too large. Remember that many schools have transportation programs available.

Then, search online for all of the schools in that geographic radius. You can use Google maps to search for schools in your area. Alternatively, there are a variety of websites listed in this section that allow you to use your address to search for schools near you. I recommend using several of these websites so that you do not miss any potential schools.

As you make your list, you will want to write down all of the schools that serve your child's grade level. Use the School Research Worksheet on page 157 as your guide. Remember that some schools serve students across many different grades.

You should include all types of schools—traditional public schools, public charter schools, magnet schools, and private schools—on this list. Do not exclude private schools because you are worried about tuition costs. Include these schools on your list, because there might be need-based, academic, or state-sponsored scholarships available.

Be sure to also include online public schools on your list, even though they do not have a fixed location. In short, do not limit your options. The goal is to create a comprehensive list. Finally, include the word "homeschooling" on your list. You never want to forget that this is an option, one that many families find incredibly successful and rewarding.

SCHOOL SEARCH WEBSITES

Great Schools
greatschools.org

National Center for Education Statistics
nces.ed.gov/ccd/schoolsearch/

Niche
niche.com/K12/

Private School Review
privateschoolreview.com

Public School Review
publicschoolreview.com

School Digger
schooldigger.com

SCHOOL RESEARCH WORKSHEET—BIG LIST

School Name	Yes	No

START NARROWING DOWN THE BIG LIST

Next, go through the list and look at the name of each school. Chances are you will know some of the schools in your area. It is possible that you have strong opinions about certain schools or have had recent personal experiences with them.

As you look at the schools on your list, you can now remove those that, for whatever reason, you will absolutely not consider under any circumstances for your child. Use your Priorities Worksheet as a guide. If you know that a school will not appropriately address one or more of your priorities, simply cross a line through the school's name. Please do not take this step lightly, and do not eliminate a school from consideration just because you heard something negative about it from one other person. Similarly, remember that schools change, for better and for worse. If you attended a school years ago, it might offer a completely different educational experience today.

Now, look at the list again. Do you have a positive, initial opinion about any of the schools based on your own recent experiences? If you do, put a star next to the name of the school. You are not ruling out the other schools that are on your list. You are just helping to set your research priorities.

START RESEARCHING THE SCHOOLS

Now, it's time to start a fresh list—one that includes all of the schools that you have not crossed out. Use the Short List Worksheet on page 160. If the worksheet in the book does not have enough room for your notes or for all of the schools you are considering, you can recreate it on a separate piece of paper or on your computer. Do not forget to include homeschooling and online schools on your new list, along with all of the other options.

Next, you will find out more information about the schools on your list. Specifically, you will want to get an initial sense of whether the schools might meet your priorities. Here are several different approaches that you can use to pursue this process:

- Visit the websites of all of the schools. Read the information on the sites, look at photos, and take notes. How does the information you discover about specific schools align to your priorities—the ones you identified on your Priorities Worksheet? If you like something about a school, write it down. If something concerns you, write it down.

- Use other sources to look up information about all of the schools. For example, you can search Google News (news. google.com) for recent news articles about the school. Look at headlines, and if something seems interesting or concerning to you, read the story and add to your notes.

- You can also look at the social media profiles and pages of all of the schools. You might consider reviewing Facebook, Twitter, YouTube, and LinkedIn. Some schools might not have social media accounts. Add any new or different information you gather from this search to your notes.

SHORT LIST WORKSHEET

School Name	Notes	Yes	Maybe	No

REFINE YOUR SHORT LIST

Now, it is time to narrow down the schools and learning environments on your Short List Worksheet. Read what you wrote about each school on your list. Then, for each school, ask yourself a simple question: Based on what I know now, will this school address my priorities and my child's needs?

If your answer is "yes," you will want to keep that school on your list. If you are leaning toward "yes" or are unsure, keep the school on the list for now. If your answer is a definite "no," cross that school off your list.

If possible, you should narrow your list down to about five to ten schools. The number of schools you are actually able to consider, in reality, will depend on where you live, the number of options available to you, and your priorities. If you cannot identify five to ten schools, that is okay. Do your best to make a manageable short list, but one that provides at least several options for your child.

But you are not done yet. Now is the time to seriously consider whether online schooling or homeschooling is right for your family. So many moms and dads have told me that even though they were nervous about starting online education or homeschooling, they rarely regretted it after they got into their own family's educational groove. Please take the Homeschooling Survey and the Online Schooling Survey at the end of this chapter. These surveys are designed to get you to think about the opportunities that these unique types of educational environments offer. If, after completing these quizzes, you believe that online schooling or homeschooling could possibly work for you, include one or both of those options on your short list, too.

After you have made your lists and taken the two surveys at the end of this step, it is time to start visiting schools and asking as many questions as possible about the learning environments that you are considering. Step Five provides a comprehensive guide for scheduling those tours, asking the right questions, and beginning the process of making your ultimate school choice decision!

HOMESCHOOLING SURVEY

The purpose of this survey is to help you consider whether homeschooling might be right for you. Circle your answers.

First Things First
Do you have the time to commit to homeschooling? This means that you or your spouse has time at home to instruct and educate your child. Remember that homeschooling families do not need to adhere to a traditional school schedule.

YES   NO

If you indicated that you do not have time to commit to homeschooling, is there a reasonable scenario in the near future in which you could have time to homeschool your children? For example, could you or your spouse take different shifts at work that would allow one of you more time?

YES   NO

Evaluation Questions
For each statement below, indicate whether you:

Strongly Agree
Agree
Are Neutral
Disagree
Strongly Disagree

I have the patience to approach homeschooling in a focused way, including asking other families or organizations for advice and suggestions if I need it.

Strongly Agree   Agree   Neutral
Disagree   Strongly Disagree

I believe that my child could respond positively to home-schooling, either now or in the future.

Strongly Agree   Agree   Neutral
Disagree   Strongly Disagree

My child could benefit from a more flexible school schedule.

Strongly Agree   Agree   Neutral
Disagree   Strongly Disagree

I believe that homeschooling could lead to higher levels of learning for my child.

Strongly Agree   Agree   Neutral
Disagree   Strongly Disagree

I believe that homeschooling could help improve or maintain my child's happiness.

Strongly Agree   Agree   Neutral
Disagree   Strongly Disagree

I believe that homeschooling could contribute positively to my child's overall success.

Strongly Agree   Agree   Neutral
Disagree   Strongly Disagree

I believe that homeschooling could be a viable way for me to address my priorities.

Strongly Agree   Agree   Neutral
Disagree   Strongly Disagree

Short Answers

Now, answer the following questions with your own short answers:

What might be the biggest benefits of homeschooling to our family?

Are there any challenges that we might encounter if we choose to homeschool?

Review Your Answers

Take a look at your answers. Do you have a lot of "Strongly Agree" or "Agree" responses to the evaluation questions? Based on your short answers, do you feel reasonably comfortable with the concept of homeschooling? If so, I encourage you to include homeschooling on your short list. Remember, this decision is entirely up to you!

The purpose of this survey is to consider whether online schooling might be right for you. Circle your answers.

First Things First

Do you have the time to commit to online schooling? For children in elementary and middle school, this means regular parental supervision. Parents of middle school and high school students may not need to provide as much real-time supervision, depending on the child's needs. Remember, online schools often offer a more flexible schedule, which allows parents and their children to customize their learning calendar.

YES   NO

Evaluation Questions

For each statement below, indicate whether you:

Strongly Agree
Agree
Are Neutral
Disagree
Strongly Disagree

I believe that my child could respond positively to online schooling, either now or in the future.

Strongly Agree   Agree   Neutral
Disagree   Strongly Disagree

My child could benefit from a more flexible school schedule.

> Strongly Agree   Agree   Neutral
> Disagree   Strongly Disagree

I believe that online schooling could lead to higher levels of learning for my child.

> Strongly Agree   Agree   Neutral
> Disagree   Strongly Disagree

I believe that online schooling could help improve or maintain my child's happiness.

> Strongly Agree   Agree   Neutral
> Disagree   Strongly Disagree

I believe that online schooling could contribute positively to my child's overall success.

> Strongly Agree   Agree   Neutral
> Disagree   Strongly Disagree

I believe that online schooling could be a viable way for me to address my priorities.

> Strongly Agree   Agree   Neutral
> Disagree   Strongly Disagree

Short Answers

Now, answer the following questions with your own short answers:

What might be the biggest benefits of online schooling to our family?

Are there any challenges that we might encounter if we choose to send our child to a full-time, online school?

Review Your Answers

Take a look at your answers. Do you have a lot of "Strongly Agree" or "Agree" responses to the evaluation questions? Based on your short answers, do you feel reasonably comfortable with the concept of online schooling? If so, I encourage you to include online schooling on your short list. Remember, this decision is entirely up to you!

step 5

VISIT SCHOOLS

YOU HAVE DONE A LOT OF WORK SO FAR. You have laid a very strong foundation for a thoughtful and effective school search process by evaluating your needs, identifying your priorities, and making and refining the list of schools in your area. You have also considered whether online schooling or home-schooling might be right for your family. Now, with your Short List Worksheet in hand, you can start visiting schools that have physical locations and meeting with school staff and teachers.

School visits and tours are an essential component to choosing a school for your child. I would never recommend that a parent choose a school for their child without a visit or tour. Reading information online and looking at pictures can tell you a lot, but it cannot paint a full portrait of a school's environment and atmosphere. Your visits are designed to help you decide if what you have read matches up with what you see, hear, and feel.

For online schools, scheduling a visit or a tour might be more challenging. But you still need to thoroughly evaluate and consider these options. You might want to look up special events, like open houses or parent nights. You can also schedule a meeting or a phone call with a representative from the school, or participate in an online presentation. Do not rule out an online school because there might not be a physical location to visit.

PLAN YOUR SCHOOL TOURS

Next, we will talk about how to schedule a school tour. The key word in that sentence is "schedule." Please do not just show up to a school and ask for a tour. For security reasons, you will likely not be permitted to enter a school if you do not have a scheduled meeting. Here are some suggestions for planning a productive school tour:

- **Visit during the school day.** If you visit a school during the school day, you can get the best sense of the environment in which your child will be learning. You will get to see teachers and students interacting with each other. For some parents, this will be challenging because most people go to work during the school day, but if you can take time off, it will be worth it. If you cannot, you can rely on a visit that is conducted when you are not working.

- **Sit in on a class or several classes.** Even if you can only sit in on one class for a few minutes, do it! Sitting in on a class will give you a sense of how students respond to a teacher and provide a snapshot of the instructional methods and strategies that are used. If you can spend a few minutes in several different classes, that is even better.

- **Bring your child.** Obviously, a school tour might not be ideal for every child. In some circumstances, parents might want to visit a school without their children. However, having your child with you on your school visit can be very beneficial. Your child might notice things about the school that you do not pick up on. Your child might also have a strong opinion about one school or another.

- **See as much of the school as possible**. A school meeting is not the same as a full tour. Sitting in a principal or counselor's office might provide you with a chance to ask questions. But you want to see as much of the school as you reasonably can. That means looking at classrooms, the lunchroom, the auditorium, and the gym. If you end up choosing this school for your child, you will want to be able to picture your child in all of these different settings.

HOW TO SCHEDULE A SCHOOL TOUR

Scheduling a school tour should not be very difficult. Just call the main office and ask for a time when you can be given a tour of the school. Here's what you could say:

> Hi, I'm _____, and I'm considering _____ for my son/daughter. I was wondering if there was a time I could schedule a tour to see the school?

Make sure to ask if you can bring your child with you. Also, ask if there is anything you need to bring with you on the tour. Some schools might ask you to send a copy of your photo identification in advance of the tour. This is for security reasons. In rare instances, a school might also ask for a proof of residence, such as a driver's license or utility bill, in advance of scheduling the visit. This usually only happens if a school is accessible only to students in a specific geographic area.

Finally, you will want to ask any logistical questions, such as where to park, who to ask for when you get to the school, and how long the tour will last.

GETTING READY FOR THE TOUR

To get ready for your tour, go back to Step One and look at the Priorities Worksheet and your Short List Worksheet to refresh your memory. If you have specific questions about a school, write them down.

For example, if you read a news article that made you question a school's approach, you might want to ask about it during your tour. Or, perhaps you want to remind yourself to ask about a specific activity that you know will be of interest to your child. I also encourage you to write some specific questions about the priorities you identified on your worksheet. You will want to bring your questions, your Priorities Worksheet, a pen and paper for notetaking, and your photo identification with you on your tours.

WHEN YOU GET TO THE SCHOOL

You will want to arrive at the school for your tour about fifteen to twenty minutes before it is supposed to begin. Finding parking or a school's main entrance can sometimes be tricky. You want to give yourself the time to figure those things out. You also want to allow enough time so that you can go through the school's security process and get checked in at the front office.

If the person who is giving you the tour—the principal, an assistant principal, an admissions staff member, or a teacher— asks you whether you want to sit down and talk first or take the tour first, opt for the tour first. Some of your questions might be answered on the tour, and the tour might lead to even more questions. You can certainly always ask questions during the tour itself, and do not be afraid to stray from the questions you have written.

DURING THE TOUR

When you're taking the tour, what exactly should you be looking at and looking for? Think of yourself as on a scavenger hunt: your goal is to collect (in your mind and in your notes) as many positive signs of learning and achievement as possible. You know better than anyone that you are not just on a tour to check out the paint colors, architecture, and decorations. While this certainly is not a comprehensive list, here are a few things you can try to notice or pay attention to on your tour:

- Do teachers have control of their classes?
- Do classes seem engaging and interesting?
- Do students appear focused on their learning?
- How do students interact with each other? Are they nice to each other?
- How do students and teachers interact with each other?

- Are staff members friendly to you in the halls, classrooms, and main office?
- Do you see books, instructional materials, and computer equipment or technology? How are they being used? Does anything stand out?
- Does the school seem orderly and organized?
- Is the building structurally sound?
- Are the temperature, lighting, noise level, and air quality acceptable to you?
- Is the school clean and well-maintained?
- Does anything impress you, concern you, or surprise you?
- Do you see signs of student achievement or accomplishments at the school—whether that means student artwork, student projects, pennants, trophies, or college acceptance letters in the office or hallways?

As you notice things that interest you, write them down. Take as many notes as you can while still focusing on your surroundings. You will want to refer to your notes later on as you evaluate all of the schools you visit.

But even as you are looking at things, listening, and taking notes, keep your focus on the most important factor: *your child*. While you are looking at schools, it can be tempting to disengage your emotions and your instincts from this process. Remember, you are not evaluating the schools you tour for *Consumer Reports* or a ratings website. You are deciding whether they will be a good fit for your child, your audience of one. So, as you tour, you need to think back to your Priorities Worksheet and keep asking yourself the following questions:

- Will my child *learn* here?
- Will my child be *safe* here?
- Will my child be *happy* here?
- Does the school foster an environment of *mutual respect*?
- Will this school help my child *succeed*?
- Does this school address or meet my other *top priorities*?
- Does this school offer the things I have identified as *specific priorities*?

WRAP UP YOUR TOUR BY ASKING QUESTIONS

After the tour, you will want to spend time talking to the person who gave you the tour. This is your opportunity, if you have not done so already, to ask your key questions—the ones you developed based on your Priorities Worksheet. Do not shy away from asking questions; school leaders usually want you to ask them questions, because they want you to make an informed and reasoned decision. In addition to the questions that you have written, here are some other questions that you might consider asking:

What is your approach to education, and what makes your school unique?

This question gives the school's representative a chance to describe their school's greatest asset or attribute—in their own words. School leaders should be able to give you a clear answer and describe the different ways that their school stands out.

What are your school's academic expectations for students?

Ask this question to let school leaders know that you are focused on your child's academic success, and that you want to talk about learning. This question will, hopefully, lead to a larger discussion of the school's approaches and methods.

What are some of the things that you do to make sure that students are learning at, or above, their grade levels?

This question will establish that you, too, have expectations for schools—while providing school leaders with opportunities to explain how they work towards accelerating student learning and success.

I want to make sure my son/daughter learns a lot. Are the classes challenging and rigorous, but also relevant and interesting?

Children can often rise to meet the challenges of rigorous coursework, if it is presented in a relevant and interesting way. Ask this question to determine how a school combines rigor and relevance, so that your child truly absorbs useful knowledge and information.

Can you please tell me what you look for when you recruit teachers? How do you define an effective teacher?

Ask this question to determine if the school has a specific approach to finding knowledgeable, talented educators whose skills align with the school's values and culture? Do school leaders consider student learning and success in determining whether teachers are effective?

How do you regularly monitor and evaluate student learning, and what do you do if students are struggling?

This question will help you find out when you will know if your child is learning at grade level, or if your child is struggling. For example, you do not want to wait a whole year to discover that your child needs extra help in a specific subject.

How do you choose your curriculum and textbooks? Do you have a specific approach?

Ask this question, because if a school uses one specific curriculum or type of textbooks for all or most of its classes, you can research it when you get home and look at examples. If the school uses several different curricula, find out how the school decides which is best.

Do your teachers use a specific instructional strategy or method? (If so, what is it called, and can you explain what that means or how that works?)

This question will help you know what, specifically, happens in a classroom. If the school uses a particular instructional strategy, ask them to explain it. For example, if you are told that the school uses "differentiated instruction," you might ask, "Can you describe how that looks day-to-day?"

Can you please tell me more about the different types of classes and activities you offer?

This question will help you determine whether the school offers the classes, clubs, activities, and sports programs that will be of interest to your child. This question will also help you identify if the school offers catch-up coursework along with advanced or gifted classes.

How do you foster an environment of mutual respect between students, teachers, and parents?

Care and respect cannot be easily measured on a test, but they should be experienced every single day in a school building. This question will help you gauge whether the school meets your standards for a caring environment and has built a culture of respect.

Please tell me more about your school's approach to keeping students safe and preventing bullying.

Ask this question to determine whether the school has specific plans, policies, and procedures that align to your goals and priorities. If you are specifically concerned about bullying, I encourage you to ask follow-up questions about this, too.

Please tell me about your school's approach to homework and testing.

Even if you do not worry too much about homework or testing, you want to make sure you know exactly what will be expected of you and your child. This question will help you get specific examples of school practices, so you can see if they align to your goals and priorities.

What are the opportunities you have for parents to be involved, and what are your expectations of parents?

By asking this question, you can determine whether a school has a thoughtful approach to parental involvement and engagement—activities that should go beyond just raising money for the school.

If you are considering online schools for your child, you can use many of these same questions during your meetings, phone conversations, or online discussions.

AFTER YOUR TOUR

After each of your tours, take a few minutes to write down any additional notes. Include anything that you want to follow up on and write down the specific things that you found exciting, interesting, concerning, or confusing about the school. It is up to you how much you want to write about each school. After touring several schools, some of the details of the schools might blend together in your mind. Your notes will help you later in the process.

BUT WHAT ABOUT HOMESCHOOLING?

If you are considering homeschooling, here are some additional steps you can take so that you can fully weigh the benefits of home education. Take some time to:

- Research the different types of curricula, books, and instruction tools you might use. There are so many different and exciting options for homeschooling families! In fact, there are more resources for homeschoolers today than at any other time in history. In the Appendix, you will find some additional resources that will help guide your research.
- Look up the different homeschool collaboratives or groups in your community. One of the most exciting parts of homeschooling is that parents and students often work together in groups, also called collaboratives. Whether you live in a big city or a small rural town, chances are there is a homeschool group near you. Find a few, call around, and meet with parents. Other parents can be incredible resources if you choose to homeschool.
- Identify whether any local schools make courses and clubs available to homeschoolers. Different states and school districts have different policies. Some schools allow homeschoolers to visit and take a course or two. Others let homeschoolers participate in clubs and on sports teams. If these are important to you, research your local policies.

TIME TO MOVE TO THE NEXT STEP

Congratulations! At this point, you have completed the most time-consuming aspects of the school search process. Hopefully, your school tours and research have been enjoyable and productive. Most importantly, I hope that you have identified several environments that might work for your child. In Step Six, you will look back at the different worksheets and exercises that you already completed—along with your notes from your school tours, interviews, and homeschooling research—so that you can effectively evaluate all of the different schools and learning environments that you are considering.

step 6

EVALUATE SCHOOLS

YOU HAVE NOW COMPLETED several assessments and exercises. You have researched and considered all types of schools, including homeschooling and online schooling. You have visited schools and taken notes. Chances are, you also have strong opinions about some of the different options you are considering. You are very close to choosing a school or learning environment for your child.

Most parents say that if they have a very strong and positive opinion about one school or learning environment after their research and tours, then this step in the process—evaluating their options—is the easiest. These families are almost ready to decide. But other parents say that if they find several good options through their research and tours, evaluating different schools and learning environments can be incredibly difficult. After all, nobody wants to make the "wrong" choice.

Regardless of what category you find yourself in, Step Six provides a good opportunity to take a step back and remind yourself of the goals you wrote for your child, as well as your priorities. To do this, you can review your Step Two Worksheet and your Priorities Worksheet, read through your notes from your school tours, and reread your research into homeschooling and online schooling.

This is also the time to conduct any additional research about the schools you are considering. Check your notes. Was there anything you wanted to research about the school's instruction strategies, methods, practices, or commitment to achievement and learning? Now is the time to search online for more answers.

You might also consider checking references by talking with other parents who send their children to the schools you have visited and are considering. Ask questions like:

- How would you describe your child's learning? Is he/she succeeding?
- Does the school provide you with regular updates about your child's academic performance?
- Are the classes interesting and engaging?
- How would you describe your child's experiences with teachers?
- Does your child feel safe and comfortable at this school?
- Is your son/daughter usually happy at this school?

- Does the school embrace the importance of mutual respect? Do they respect your involvement and engagement as a parent?
- What do you wish you knew about this school that you didn't know when you picked it?
- What is one thing I should watch out for, if anything, if I choose this school?
- What do you think is the best thing about this school?

Your goal will be to identify trends—similar things that several people tell you. Remember—and I know, I am a broken record about this—your child's experiences at a school might be completely different than another child's experiences.

Then, after you have conducted additional research online and talked with other parents, you should narrow down your list of schools to three, using the Evaluation Questionnaire on page 186. The questionnaire includes questions that are customized to your priorities. The answer to each of these questions is the name of the school or learning environment you are considering. Write each answer in the first line and list the second-best answer on the second line. Please make sure that you remember homeschooling and any online schools that you are considering as you complete this questionnaire.

After completing the questionnaire, you will hopefully have narrowed your list of schools or learning environments down to three. You can then proceed to Step Seven.

EVALUATION QUESTIONNAIRE

What school or learning environment will best inspire and motivate my child to be the person that I hope he or she will be?

1. _____
2. _____

What school or learning environment best reflects my family's overall values, goals, and principles?

1. _____
2. _____

What school or learning environment best meets my expectations for what a school should be able to do for my child?

1. _____
2. _____

What school or learning environment would do the most to alleviate my biggest worries or concerns for my child's future?

1. _____
2. _____

What school or learning environment will do the most to help my child learn and succeed academically?

    1. _____
    2. _____

What school or learning environment do I think is the safest environment for my child?

    1. _____
    2. _____

What school or learning environment best embraces the importance of mutual respect?

    1. _____
    2. _____

What school or learning environment will best maximize, maintain, or improve my child's happiness?

    1. _____
    2. _____

What school or learning environment will best promote my child's overall success?

    1. _____
    2. _____

What school or learning environment best meets my needs in regard to the other top priorities that I identified as mattering most to me?

1. _____
2. _____

What school or learning environment best meets my needs in regard to the other specific priorities that I identified as mattering most to me?

1. _____
2. _____

Do you notice a trend? Are there schools that consistently appear as your first answer to these questions? Use your answers here to narrow down your list to three finalists.

Remember, your gut reaction matters, too. If, for any reason, your intuition tells you that a school might not work for your child, strike it off the list and stop considering it. Even if it might technically meet a lot of the criteria for you, if it doesn't feel right, it isn't right.

YOUR FINALISTS

1. _____
2. _____
3. _____

step 7

CHOOSE THE SCHOOL OR LEARNING ENVIRONMENT THAT MEETS YOUR CHILD'S NEEDS

YOU HAVE REACHED THE FINAL STEP in the school choice process. You are ready to make a decision and apply for, or enroll your child at, the school or learning environment of your choice. Choosing between your three finalists is an incredibly personal decision. At this point, you have gone through many different rounds of evaluation and consideration. It is time to let your intuition be your guide.

Before we talk about how to make your final choice, here are two ways that you can approach this final step:

- The first way is to apply for enrollment at all three finalist schools and then make a decision. In some cities and school districts, parents who are considering multiple public sector schools (including traditional public schools, public charter schools, magnet schools, and online schools) can prioritize their preferences on a "common application," which is described more thoroughly in the Frequently Asked Questions section at the end of Part Two. Even if you do not live in a city or school district that allows you to apply to multiple schools using one form or application, it might be a good idea to apply to all of the schools on your shortlist—using each school's application form—at the same. If you apply to multiple schools, you will still have options, even if there are no seats available at your first-choice school. You will also avoid missing deadlines. Finally, private schools sometimes offer scholarship information only after students have formally applied.

- The second way is to simply enroll your child, or apply for their enrollment, at your first-choice school or learning environment. This option works best for parents who like their neighborhood public school the best, are choosing a charter or magnet school with seats available, or are confident that their children will be accepted into a private school and that they will be able to afford the tuition either through their own funds, through a school-based scholarship, through a local scholarship organization, or through a state-sponsored scholarship program. This option also works effectively for parents who have chosen to homeschool their children and want to get the homeschooling process started.

Whether you are making your ultimate decision before you apply or enroll—or after your child has been accepted—you should follow the same process and identify the school that is your first choice.

To do this, you want to first talk as a family. Discuss every aspect of the schools and learning environments on your list of finalists. Depending on your child's age, consulting with your child on this decision can be helpful. However, asking your child's opinion on different types of schools, or asking about the pros and cons of schools and learning environments, may be more productive than indicating to your child that he or she will be making the choice by himself or herself. While some parents might trust their children to decide between two good choices, other families have specific values and priorities that their children might not fully appreciate or understand. As the parent, this is *your* decision. As you talk, trust your intuition. Ask yourselves questions such as:

- Can we envision our child succeeding at this school or learning environment? If so, why?
- Does this option provide an environment that truly meets all or most of our top priorities and specific priorities?
- What concerns do we have about this school or learning environment, and how serious are these concerns?

This conversation should lead to a decision: the choice of where you want to send your child to school or if you want your child educated online or at home.

APPLYING AND ENROLLING

Once you have made your choice, you need to apply or enroll in the school, unless you have done so already. Every school is different, and you will have received enrollment information when you visited the school.

As you complete the paperwork, make sure to follow the instructions very carefully, and call the school if you have any questions before submitting it. You do not want to accidentally complete a form incorrectly and then find out that you have missed a deadline. If you are submitting an application online rather than on paper, you might want to call and make sure your application has been received. Do not let a computer error or internet mix-up derail your school enrollment process.

If you have chosen to homeschool your child, you will want to make sure you follow all of the steps necessary, as required by your state's laws, to comply with the rules. After all the information and documents are completed, make sure the appropriate state or school district official has received them.

AFTER YOU CHOOSE

Congratulations! You have reached the end of the seven-step process of choosing a school or learning environment for your child. Hopefully, you have also received answers to many of your questions. You can feel comfortable and confident knowing that you have done everything possible to evaluate your needs, research your choices, consider every possible school option, and pursue a thoughtful, deliberative process toward making a short list and an ultimate decision.

So, what is next? Hopefully, your child will soon be enrolled in the school or learning environment of your choice and is getting ready to start his or her first day. In some cases, that might be at a physical school building. In other cases, that learning might take place online or at home.

After you have completed the school search process, I hope you will spend just as much time working with your child on the transition to a new school or learning environment as you did searching for the school. Finding a school is not the end of the journey. It is just the beginning. If your child has struggled in his or her previous school, catching up on learning will take time.

One way you can start this transition is by talking with your child about what he or she can expect. If you are sending your child to a school with a physical location, sit down and talk about the school and its expectations for your child. Set your own expectations, too, so that your child truly understands that you care about his or her success. But at the same time, do not portray education as simply a set of expectations or boxes that a child must check in order to move on to adulthood. Be supportive and encouraging, and talk about all of the opportunities that the school or education option will offer your child. If you have chosen homeschooling, this step is just as important. Children need to understand that learning in the home will be separate and different from just relaxing at home, and they need to understand the difference between learning and doing chores.

You can also use this conversation to start an open dialogue with your child about his or her education. Tell your child that you want to know all of the good things that happen at school or in your child's new learning environment, as well as the things that might concern or worry your child. Set those benchmarks and open the door to future conversations so that you and your child can talk openly and honestly about his or her education and experiences. Most importantly, answer any questions that your child has.

For many parents, this conversation will not be too difficult or lengthy, as your children will likely have been involved in the school selection process. However, school leaders that I talk to tell me that one of the best indicators of a child's initial success at school is their understanding of what to expect from that learning environment. Children who have a better understanding of what they are getting into tend to acclimate better.

Starting an open and productive discussion with the principal and teachers at your child's school and developing relationships with other families is also helpful. Starting these discussions on a positive note, and not just waiting to talk to school leaders, teachers, or other parents when there are problems, will help you to anticipate challenges and, hopefully, prevent some of them.

Part of this dialogue includes reading all of the materials and communications that a school sends to you, participating in parent-teacher conferences, and making sure that you know how your child is doing in his or her classes. If you have chosen to homeschool your child, it is often very helpful to get involved with your local homeschooling organization.

Encouraging your children to participate in extracurricular activities, clubs, or sports can also help smooth the transition to a new school or learning environment. School leaders and teachers frequently say—and research backs this up—that when students find extracurricular activities that interest and motivate them, they have a better chance at success in school. It is important to note that this success does not necessarily grow with the number of activities a child pursues. Simply finding one or two things that are inspirational can make a difference.

Finally, you can help ease your child's transition to a new school by building an environment of learning, discovery, and exploration outside of school. Regardless of whether you read together as a family, visit free museums, take weekend trips to historic sites, discover nature at local parks, or take your children to work to show them what you do for a living, building a culture of learning and discovery will help to reinforce the importance that you, as a parent, place on education. Throughout this process, your child will learn, grow, thrive, and succeed. And hopefully, your active choice of a learning environment for your child will lead to greater happiness for your entire family.

"Encourage and involve your children in the choices of their education; help them keep a positive mindset about education. It is their future and there are no limits to what they can accomplish. School choice gives them the power to be more responsible regarding that future. Ask them often what they like and what they want to be. Let them know it is okay when or if their ideas change along the way."

KIMBERLEY, A MOTHER FROM SIMPSONVILLE, SOUTH CAROLINA

"Sometimes making the transition into a new environment can be scary and intimidating for a student. Be supportive and help them to understand that the choice of education is being made for their continued growth and success. Speak frequently with the chosen school's teachers, administrators, and guidance counselors to make sure any and all of your child's learning needs can and will be accommodated."

WENDY, A MOTHER FROM EAST ORANGE, NEW JERSEY

"Know your child. What are their strengths and weaknesses? Do they need accommodations? What is the interest of your child? What values do you want your child taught? Check out all available options. Don't be shy about asking questions. This is your child and you want the best for him or her!"

KENNETH, A FATHER FROM TYLER, TEXAS

"I would suggest choosing the environment where they are happy and safe. Are they getting the individualized help that they may need? Or are they becoming agitated and experiencing changes in their behavior? These are the exact questions that my family had to answer to determine where our children would thrive. Only you, the parent, know what is best for your children."

LAUREN, A MOTHER FROM BAKERSVILLE, NORTH CAROLINA

frequently asked questions

THROUGHOUT YOUR SCHOOL SEARCH PROCESS, you are likely to have additional questions. While I have attempted to address potential questions throughout the chapters of this book, I wanted to make sure that answers to other common questions are easy to reference, too. This chapter provides answers to frequently asked school choice questions on topics that require more detailed or comprehensive answers. For additional website links and information regarding these questions, please visit schoolchoiceroadmap.com.

What schools are required to provide services to
children with special learning needs or disabilities?

Children with special learning needs or disabilities often require an individualized approach to learning to maximize their chances at success.

If your child has special learning needs, you likely already know that you must be his or her fiercest advocate. Services and education for children with special needs vary by state, but all public sector schools are required to follow a federal law called the Individuals with Disabilities Education Act (IDEA).[69] IDEA has established the following six broad criteria that all public sector schools must meet:

- Public sector schools must provide a "Free Appropriate Public Education" (FAPE) for children with disabilities. If they cannot do this, they must find an alternative or private educational setting for your child.
- Public sector schools must allow for appropriate evaluations of students. These evaluations must be conducted in a professional way and are designed to determine whether your child qualifies for special education services.
- Public sector schools must write an Individualized Education Plan (IEP) for your child. An IEP is a roadmap that details the different ways the school will work to help your child succeed.
- Public sector schools must do everything possible to not restrict your child's education. This means the school must actively work to make sure that as many children with disabilities as possible are able to participate in classroom activities.
- Public sector schools must include you, the parent, in their

decision making. IDEA requires schools to allow parents to be equal partners in their children's education. This means many different things, including that parents must be included in meetings regarding their children's education.

- Public sector schools must ensure that parents have the opportunity to get information about their children's education and appeal decisions or determinations that are made regarding their children's education.

For all schools in the public sector, IDEA must be followed. That includes traditional public schools, public charter schools, public magnet schools, and online public schools. According to the U.S. Department of Education, schools "generally may not ask a prospective student if he or she has a disability," unless the student is applying to a school that is specifically designed to serve children with special needs.[70] Additionally, once a student is enrolled in a school, the school is not permitted to "counsel out, i.e., try to convince a student (or parents) that the student should not attend (or continue to attend) the school because the student has a disability."[71]

IDEA does not apply to private schools. However, that does not mean that private schools do not serve children with special needs. In fact, many do. In a variety of states, public sector schools that cannot provide children with FAPE pay to send children to private schools that are specifically designed to serve children with disabilities. These situations are commonly referred to as "outplacements." An increasing number of states now allow parents of children with special needs to use state-funded scholarship programs to send their children to these schools without first requiring them to get permission from a school district. As a result, private schools are playing an essential role in helping provide a quality, effective education for children with special needs.

Regardless of the type of school you are considering, I encourage you to ask questions to make sure that you are comfortable with the school's educational approach when it comes to special needs. Here are just some of the questions you could ask:

- Does your school have experience educating children with my child's specific disability/difference/need?
- What is your approach to educating children with my child's specific disability/difference/need?
- How have other students with special needs succeeded here?
- What type of accommodations are frequently made for children with special needs?
- How will you keep me informed of my child's education and development?
- What other resources does the school offer for families of children with special needs?

What types of schools require school uniforms?

School uniforms often make parents think of private education. Indeed, many private schools require uniforms. However, there are traditional public schools, public charter schools, and public magnet schools that require uniforms. According to the NCES, approximately 21.5 percent of all public sector schools now require school uniforms.[72] There are also schools in all sectors that do not require uniforms. If you are interested in a school that requires uniforms or a stricter dress code, be sure to ask about the school's uniform policy or dress code during your school visit. You should also consider asking who is responsible for paying for the uniforms, how much they cost, and how a lost or damaged uniform can be replaced.

How should I evaluate a school's test scores or rating?

For schools in the public sector, you can usually find out how students in the school are performing on standardized tests or assessments. For example, there are a variety of websites that provide information on the percentage of students in each public sector school who are proficient in state-mandated math, English, and science tests, and compare schools' data to state averages. Some states even grade or rate public sector schools. Many private schools also provide similar information to prospective parents. However, private school data is not usually available on school rating websites.

Do these scores matter, and how should you read them? First, it is important to remember that one year of test scores only provides a snapshot of how that year's students performed on tests. It does not take into account any changes that a school might have made after those scores were posted. Here's an analogy to illustrate this: When we do projects at home, we often like to look at before-and-after pictures, not just before *or* after pictures. Imagine if you took a photo of a garden before you planted it with seeds and bulbs. It would not look like much of a garden. Weeks or months later, however, after you've planted and watered it, another snapshot would show an actual garden.

If you are concerned about how students in a school perform on standardized tests, I encourage you to look at how much progress the students in that school are making from year to year. This allows you to avoid basing your decision on a snapshot alone, basing it instead on a more accurate before-and-after picture. I also encourage you to look at other factors, in addition to test scores. For example, you can consider high school graduation rates, or find out the percentage of students who move on to their next grade or level of education.

Most importantly, I also encourage you to ask schools about their academic results. If you are concerned about anything that you saw or read about a school's performance, please remember to ask about it during your school visit. If you think that a school is struggling, or has struggled in the past, ask specific questions to determine how the school is working to improve.

Should I make sure a school has received accreditation?

School accreditation can be a challenging topic to navigate. Because there are many different organizations that provide accreditation to schools, the value of a school's accreditation depends on the reputation of the accreditor.

Many public sector and private sector schools go through rigorous processes to earn and maintain accreditation from widely respected organizations and associations. In those cases, accreditation can be a valid indicator that a school has met specific benchmarks for success. However, some accreditations and accrediting bodies may be less rigorous.

In some states, the law requires public sector schools, or public school districts, to earn accreditation. Other states have accreditation requirements for private schools, too. The U.S. Department of Education provides information about these policies in two reports that are available online, *Accreditation and Quality Assurance: School-Level Accreditation* and *State Regulations of Private Schools.* In states that require accreditation, it may be easier to identify whether a school's accreditation should be considered in your search process, as the state has usually approved specific accrediting agencies in an attempt to weed out those that do not meet baseline standards.

In states that do not require accreditation, it is important to note that there are popular schools that do not pursue accreditation, and some that do. A school may have a long track record of success and see no need to pursue accreditation.

If you are curious about accreditation, ask about it. For example, if you are worried that a high school's lack of accreditation may impact your child's chances of being accepted to colleges, ask about the school's college acceptance rate and process. If you have questions about a school's accreditor, take some time and research the organization that issued the accreditation. Also, if this really matters to you, watch out for different terminology, like registration, licensure, and approval. These terms are different than accreditation. Finally, remember that an accreditation will not guarantee your child's success in a school.

How do I make sure that a school has
certified or qualified teachers?

Parents occasionally ask me about the importance of teacher certification or licensure. Is it important for a school to have teachers who are certified? After working for several years in the field of public school teacher recruitment and certification, I can tell you that the answer to this question is complicated, because states have so many different types and levels of certifications. Nonprofit organizations have literally developed massive flowcharts and maps to help make sense of the different teacher certification policies in different states.

The general consensus, however, is that it is important to have teachers who have strong knowledge in their subject areas, who understand teaching strategies, and who have passed background checks. You also want to find a school where teachers are caring and respectful. Teachers can meet these criteria with or without certification.

In most states, certification sets specific benchmarks that teachers need to meet to *enter* the classroom or *stay in* a classroom. These usually require teachers to hold bachelor's degrees, pass background checks, take subject matter tests, perform student teaching or mentoring, or take special online or college courses. Many of these items are important. However, certification is not always a "stamp of approval" that indicates that a state or school district has evaluated a teacher after that teacher is already in the classroom and believes that he or she is effective.

Almost all teachers in traditional public schools, public charter schools, public magnet schools, and online public schools are required to have some level of certification. Sometimes, these certifications are issued on a temporary, probationary, emergency, or provisional basis, depending on the teacher's situation and the school's needs. As a result, it is relatively easy for schools to say that all of their teachers are certified.

In most states, private school teachers are not required to be certified by the state. Schools can develop their own certification or licensure programs and determine how they want to evaluate effective instruction. There are also private organizations that provide certification services for private school teachers.

As you consider schools, ask about teacher *qualifications* rather than solely focusing on *certification*. If you are concerned about teacher qualifications, here are the questions that I would ask:

- Are all staff members required to undergo background checks?
- How do you evaluate teachers at your school?
- How you find teachers with the right content knowledge and experience?
- How long do teachers usually stay working at this school?

Those questions will hopefully get you the answers that you are looking for without getting too technical.

What is a common application?

Some cities and school districts offer a process that allows parents to apply to several schools for their children at the same time—by filling out one common application. These applications can be helpful, as they allow parents to focus more on the choices they are making than on filling out the forms.

All common applications are different. A city or school district might have a common application that follows a completely different process than that of another district.

For example, some common applications allow parents to apply to *all* public sector schools, including traditional public schools, public charter schools, public magnet schools, and online schools. Other common applications are provided only for traditional public schools or only for charter schools. Some common applications include private schools, too. And still other common applications allow you to apply to only the schools that have opted to participate in the application process.

After you fill out and complete a common application, individual schools will let you know whether your child has been accepted to attend those schools or whether they have been waitlisted. In some instances, filling out a common application is part of a unified enrollment system, which is described in the answer to the next question.

If a common application process is available in your area, here are some questions I encourage you to ask before you complete and submit a common application:

- Is the common application required?
- Is the common application part of a unified enrollment system?
- Which schools participate in this application?
- What information do I need to complete the application?
- What deadlines must I meet?
- When will I find out if my child has been accepted to schools?
- What do I need to do after my child has been accepted to schools?

What are unified enrollment systems, and do these application
systems require a different school search process?

Some larger public school districts have developed processes—
called *unified enrollment systems*—that are designed to help
facilitate school choice. These processes allow or require all
parents in the district to fill out common applications. On these
applications, parents identify the public sector schools that they
would prefer for their children, usually ranking them in order
of preference. After all the applications from parents are col-
lected by the district—and the district officials determine which
schools are most in demand—the district uses algorithms and
lottery systems to assign the children to schools. Ideally, each
child will be assigned to one of the schools that their parents
identified as their top choices.

In addition to reducing paperwork burdens for families,
these systems provide important information to school districts
and charter school authorizers. If some types of schools prove
incredibly popular and continue to have wait lists, a school
district might want to consider expanding or replicating those
schools to meet the demand.

However, these systems are not without their challenges. For
example, in a system with unified enrollment, parents must be
vigilant about making sure that they do not miss application
deadlines. Missing a deadline could mean missing out on not
just one school that they like, but many of them.

Is there a trick to ranking your preferred schools in a unified
enrollment system? In short, no. I recommend ranking schools
on a unified enrollment application in the same way that you
ranked them in Part Two. I would be wary of anyone who offers

you advice on a "strategy" to somehow gain an advantage on a unified application by including schools that are not on your list.

What should I do if the school I have chosen does not have space available or if my child is placed on a wait list?

Imagine that you have completed all of the steps in the school search process, found a school that sounds like the perfect fit for your child, and applied. Then, you find out that the school is full, or that more students applied to enroll in the school than there are places available.

What do you do next? That depends on the type of school. If you are enrolling your child in a public sector school, you should ask if and when there will be a random lottery to determine which children will be selected for the school. In public charter schools, public magnet schools, and online public schools, the school must usually conduct a random lottery to determine who enters it if more students apply to attend than there are seats available. Traditional public schools generally do not have wait lists if you select a school within your zone. However, wait list and lottery policies vary by state.

There are occasionally some exceptions to the "randomness" of the lottery process. Depending on your state, some schools are allowed, for example, to give preference to students whose siblings already attend the school. If your child is not accepted through the lottery process, he or she may still remain on the school's wait list to be considered in a future lottery. In that case, you need to make a decision: do you want to enroll your child in your second choice school and try to make it work? Do you want to enroll your child in your second choice school and see if the wait list clears? Or, do you want to reconsider your options entirely?

This is up to you, and each family will make its own choice. Ask questions about wait lists as you evaluate and consider schools. Prepare yourself for this possibility.

If you are trying to enroll your child in a private school and discover there is a wait list, the situation might be different. Private schools have their own policies for addressing and clearing wait lists. I recommend calling the school and asking if they can provide more information or even offer an exception. It always helps your child's chances of being accepted to show your enthusiasm for a school. Regardless of how you handle a wait list or lottery situation, these situations are never easy.

How can a parent navigator organization help me?

In some cities, there are specific nonprofit organizations that help parents navigate the school search process. These organizations can be incredibly beneficial and supportive, and they provide their services to parents at no cost. These organizations—sometimes referred to as parent navigator organizations—provide assistance in school applications, school tours, and transportation questions, among other things. They also help parents navigate wait list scenarios. If there is a parent navigator organization in your area and you believe you would benefit from these types of services, I encourage you to work with one.

According to Colleen Dippel, who runs parent navigator

organization Families Empowered serving families in Houston, Austin, and San Antonio, Texas, these organizations focus on practical ways to provide immediate support to families. "We want people to reach out to us any time they are looking for a school. We encourage people to start this process early—early in a child's life and early in the year, too," she says. "Our most impactful services are a live call-in center and text messaging support, in addition to school fairs and application nights. Some of the most important information we offer is not just about *how to choose a school* or the *types of schools available,* but the mechanics of the process. Deadlines are important, and all common applications are different."

As for providing one-on-one advice to families searching for schools and learning environments, Dippel's organization advises that every family's situation is different. "Your school preferences might change based on what you learn about the options available. We want parents to keep their children's needs at the forefront of their minds at all times." Dippel says that her organization encourages parents not to focus on only one piece of data or advice alone when considering a school or learning environment—whether such data is taken from a school's ranking or such advice is that of a single "maven mom." "We encourage parents to constantly ask themselves, 'What is in the best interests of my child,' to remember that a child's needs change over time, and to take school tours," she says.

For states and localities without parent navigator organizations like Families Empowered, Dippel recommends that parents seek advice from local organizations that they trust, from their children's pediatricians, or from broad circles of their friends and family members who have a wide array of experiences with different schools and types of schools.

How do I find a scholarship so that I can
send my child to private school?

There are several different types of scholarships available to students who want to attend private school. Schools frequently offer academic or need-based scholarships, primarily to students whose parents cannot afford tuition costs. Local organizations or religious entities may also offer scholarships. Your first step toward identifying scholarships should be to ask the school you have chosen or are considering. Schools will often readily share information about scholarship opportunities, especially if there are organizations in the area that offer scholarships. Some national organizations, such as the Children's Scholarship Fund and ACE Scholarships, also offer K-12 scholarships to students.

In twenty-nine states and the District of Columbia, there are also state-sponsored programs that provide scholarships for students who want to attend private schools. Generally, these programs are offered for children from low-income or middle-income families, or for children who have special learning needs. These scholarships have many different names. Some are called *opportunity scholarships,* while others are called *tax credit scholarships, tuition tax deductions,* or *education savings accounts.* Some programs are simply referred to as *private school choice* programs.

If you plan to apply for a need-based scholarship, particularly one that is sponsored by a state, be prepared to provide information on your family's annual income and expenses. This usually includes some of the same data that you document on your state and federal tax returns. You can learn more about these programs on the websites of EdChoice at edchoice.org and the American Federation for Children at federationforchildren.org.

At the federal level, there are no federal government scholarships currently available for families who want to send their children to private schools. However, parents can now save money for K-12 private school tuition in tax deferred accounts called 529 plans. If you invest post-tax money in a 529 plan, you will not be taxed on the growth of the money within that plan.[73]

I want to homeschool, but I don't know where to start. What should I do?

If you have gone through the process of choosing a school or education environment for your child and determined that homeschooling would work best for your child, you might be nervous or uncertain when you first start the process. This is completely normal. But parents who homeschool their children tell me that these worries generally melt away once you get into the homeschooling groove.

The first step is to make sure you understand your state's laws and rules. Write those rules and policies down, or print them out, and keep them handy. You want to make sure you are in compliance. After that, I encourage you to take stock of the resources, curricula, and instructional materials that are available to you to help you through this process. A statewide homeschool organization or website can point you in the right direction. You should also work to find a local homeschooling group, collaborative, or collective. These groups, which are comprised of local homeschooling families, will provide support and assistance to you.

Finally, as Elissa Wahl from the RISE Resource Center in Nevada told me, new homeschoolers should remember that the first year of homeschooling is always the hardest. You are still figuring things out, and your child is still getting acclimated to being educated in the home.

Can homeschooling families access extracurricular activities and sports programs at nearby public schools?

When parents choose homeschooling, they are taking the responsibility of educating their children fully into their own hands. But these parents also pay the same local, state, and federal taxes as all other families—taxes that go to support local public schools.

Because of this, some homeschooling families understandably want their children to be able to participate in the sports and extracurricular activities offered within the traditional public school system. Over the past decade, progress has been made to expand this type of access. In almost half of U.S. states, school districts are required to allow homeschooled children to participate in extracurricular, interscholastic, and sports activities.[74] In other states, homeschoolers may be permitted to participate in activities and classes, but some limitations or restrictions apply.

How does the high school I choose for my child impact
his or her ability to get accepted into college?

The college admissions process can be complicated. For years, many parents worried that if they chose certain high schools for their children, or if they homeschooled, their kids would have a tougher time getting into certain colleges.

As more families have actively chosen schools for their children, most colleges and universities have changed their admissions policies to welcome students from a broader variety of educational backgrounds.

Certainly, some Ivy League schools still enroll a large number of students from so-called "feeder" schools. These schools are usually elite private schools or selective public sector high schools. However, students from all types of schools, along with homeschooled students, are still regularly accepted into America's most prestigious colleges and universities.

Generally speaking, colleges do not simply eliminate students from consideration because they attended certain schools or pursued education through one specific type of school or learning environment. Instead, they look at a student's performance at a school, and they look at that performance in the context of different characteristics of the school. Other factors, such as your child's Scholastic Aptitude Test (SAT) or American College Testing (ACT) scores, his or her grades in high school, and the types of coursework your child pursued in school, are likely to matter more to a college than the specific high school that he or she attended.

As I write this, there are two developments that have the potential to change the landscape of the college admissions process. One of these is the bribery scandal, where some wealthy parents (outrageously) gamed the college admissions system to make it easier to get their children accepted into selective colleges.[75] The other is a proposal by the College Board, which administers the SAT, to append a hardship score to each student who takes the test. This score takes into account a child's neighborhood, family income, and other factors.[76] The College Board says that this score will help even the playing field in college admissions, but skeptics—including the organization that administers the ACT—are concerned that the adversity score will lead to more colleges simply looking at data rather than at the merits of individual students.[77]

Regardless, if you are concerned about your child's chances at getting accepted to a specific college or to a more selective college, ask questions about these matters during your school visits. The representatives at the high schools you are visiting should be able to answer the following questions:

- Can you tell me how many students from here applied and got accepted to colleges?
- Which colleges are the most popular for students who go to this school?
- What services or support do you offer to help students in the college admissions process?
- Have students from this school been accepted to selective colleges or universities?

Most importantly, though, do not choose a high school that does not fit your child's needs simply because you think it might give you an edge in college admissions. This type of approach can do more harm than good, as it can increase the odds that your child will not succeed in school. To gain a more thorough answer to this question, consult someone with detailed knowledge of the college admissions process.

How do I resolve a specific problem at/with my child's school (and when should I consider finding a different environment)?

Parents frequently ask me how to address problems at their children's schools. The answer to this question depends on the severity of the problems that families are experiencing. Here are several categories that will help you classify your concerns:

- Situations that are extreme and pose a danger to your child's physical or emotional well-being. These situations include persistent bullying that has gone unaddressed, or a fear of violence or mistreatment at a school.

- Situations that are serious in which you feel that your child's academic progress or development is suffering in his or her current school or your child's all-around happiness is negatively impacted either by a school setting or an unsupportive or disrespectful school environment.

- Situations that represent specific concerns related to a class, subject, teacher, or activity in a school. These situations are usually ones in which a parent and child have a generally positive experience with a school, but a specific incident or bad experience has caused concern.

- Situations that are annoyances. For example, you might not like the school's lunch program, you might think that the school holds too many fundraisers, or you may not like the way that a school conducts field trips.

If you feel that your child is in immediate physical or emotional danger, you might want to find an alternative environment immediately, while you evaluate all of the options available for your child's education. If no options exist, you need to address the problem with determination and a sense of urgency. Be persistent, escalate the situation, and be very reluctant to ever take "sorry, there is nothing we can do" for an answer.

A few years ago, I received a random call from a South Florida father who had watched an interview I conducted on national television. He told me that his son was suicidal because of persistent bullying in school. He was evaluating his other school choice options but wanted to address the bullying in the interim. This father had talked to the principal at his son's school about the situation, but the bullying continued. I encouraged him to contact the school district's superintendent, and if that did not work, to contact every member of the district's school board. Within two weeks, his son's situation improved.

While this situation may seem extreme, the seeming increase in bullying has made those types of scenarios more common. I have talked to more than a few parents of children whose sense of self—and, in some cases, will to live—have been impacted by this type of behavior.

For situations that do not rise to the level of physical or emotional danger, I also recommend a persistent approach. I occasionally hear from parents whose children are in second, third, or fourth grade and still cannot read. These challenges are absolutely serious. I encourage you to schedule meetings with your child's teachers and principal. In these meetings, ask specific questions and seek specific solutions. If those meetings do not work, continue escalating while searching for a different education environment.

There are some serious situations that meetings might not fix. If your son or daughter is persistently unhappy in a school, the school simply might not be a good environment for them. Talk to your child and try to get at the root of the problem and see what accommodations the school can make while you consider another environment.

Some problems are less severe but still need to be addressed. These are specific concerns. For example, what if your child is generally doing well in school but is having a really tough time with one subject? In that case, you might be able to just address the situation with the teacher and work to develop a plan to get your son or daughter up to speed.

For things that are simply annoying, you should weigh the pros and cons of addressing the situation. Chances are, unless the annoyance turns into a more serious problem, it is unlikely that you will need to change schools. Accordingly, your approach to addressing the situation should be more measured.

As you consider whether to address a problem or to switch schools, remember that your intuition as a parent should always be your north star. Trust your intuition, listen to your child, and make the best decision for your child and his or her future.

How can I help to improve the school my child attends?

Unfortunately, some parents may find that their child's current school is not a good fit. After speaking with other families, they might also discover that those parents have concerns, too. What should you do if you cannot find another school or learning environment for your child? How can you and other families improve the school your child attends so that it works better for your child and even other children?

To provide a truly effective answer to this question, I would need to write an entirely different book. Indeed, other handbooks and online articles have been published to provide families with information on improving their children's schools. There are also dozens of local, state, and national organizations that have been set up to help improve schools of all types. You can find some of them listed in the Appendix.

If you want to help make meaningful improvements to your child's school, I encourage you to work with other parents and *be vocal*. When parents work together, especially in partnership with educators, community leaders, and policymakers, things happen more quickly than if one parent stands alone. You can meet with teachers and administrators, speak at public meetings, and be persistent in your desire for change. As you work to improve your child's school, here are some things that I hope you will consider:

- *Talk with teachers.* Teachers often have many good ideas for how to improve schools that are struggling. But in some schools, teachers do not have enough freedom to make bigger decisions that could benefit their students and their classrooms. Talk with teachers and find out if there are things they wish they could do. If these things make sense to you, talk with school leaders and see if you can encourage them to give teachers more flexibility to implement these new ideas.

- *Work toward immediate changes first.* Every day that a child does not succeed in a school can be detrimental. You should work along with teachers and other parents to identify and recommend immediate and low-cost changes that can improve your child's school. This will help build momentum for even greater changes. Even seemingly small changes, like adding different activities, creating study clubs, changing the start of a school day, changing the school's dress code or discipline policy, altering the school's homework policy, or creating better methods for parents to communicate with teachers, might be helpful.

- *Ask if the school can try a new instructional strategy.* Sometimes, a school may be using an instructional strategy or method that is not working for many of its students. For example, if you discover that the school relies a lot on group work and most students still seem to struggle, you might ask that the school consider adopting a teaching strategy that focuses more on direct instruction. Talk with teachers and administrators about the options that the school might pursue.

- *Create an independent parent organization to help improve the school—and not just for fundraising purposes.* If your child attends a school that struggles to educate too many of its students, see if other parents will work with you to help the school. Whether you develop an after-school study club, develop programs to help teachers, create new activities to help students improve their learning, or work to raise awareness in your community about the need for school improvements, an independent parent organization can be helpful. Effective parent organizations allow for meaningful involvement. They do not just ask moms and dads to sell things and raise money for the school.

- *Involve the community.* Building community support for making improvements to a school can be very helpful. Even more helpful is when local businesses, civic leaders, and other organizations provide advice, make recommendations, and get involved in helping a school to succeed. Every school plays an important role in its community. By making people feel truly invested in the success of your child's school, you can help accelerate the pace of change.

Regardless of which strategies and tactics you pursue to improve your child's school, I encourage you to be persistent. Remember that, if successful, your efforts will benefit not only your child but also many other children in the future. As you work to improve your child's school, you should also consider working to expand the school choice options in your community and state. Remember that one school will not work for every student and that options are essential toward building a diverse and effective educational climate in a community.

How can I work to expand school choice
options in my community or state?

Some families will unfortunately discover that there are not nearly enough choices in their communities and states. These families often ask me how they can be a part of the effort to expand school choice. Some parents want to work toward expanding open enrollment programs, while others want more public charter schools, more magnet schools, better access to online public schools, the creation of state-supported private school choice programs, more opportunities for homeschooling families to participate in publicly funded school activities, or all of the above. All of the school choice options available in America today are the direct result of parents taking action to encourage state legislators to expand opportunities in K-12 education.

I encourage you to get involved. The vast majority of school choice policies are decided at the state level by state lawmakers and legislators, not by individual school districts, school boards, or the federal government. You can search for a local or state-wide organization that promotes and encourages education reform, link up with a national organization that supports different types of school choice, or create your own grassroots parent group. You can find a variety of school choice advocacy and support organizations listed in the Appendix of this book.

How do I get involved in National School Choice Week?

National School Choice Week (NSCW) is America's largest annual public awareness effort designed to let parents know about the K-12 education options available for their children. It's also the effort I run, so it gets a special and well-deserved shout-out in this book! NSCW provides an opportunity for parents to research schools and learning environments for their children, and it provides schools with a chance to celebrate what makes them unique.

Held every January, NSCW features tens of thousands of events and activities. These events and activities include school fairs, information sessions, parent nights, and school-based celebrations. They are independently planned by schools, homeschool groups, organizations, and individuals. Over the past nine years, more than 131,000 NSCW events have been planned across the country and around the world. NSCW recognizes all K-12 options, including traditional public schools, public charter schools, public magnet schools, private schools, online schools, and homeschooling. NSCW is a nonpartisan, nonpolitical, independent public awareness effort. It is not associated with any legislative lobbying or advocacy.

You can get involved in NSCW by using the week to search for a school or learning environment for your child. Or, if you've found a school or learning environment that is working for your child, use NSCW to spread the word. Thank your child's teachers, write positive social media posts about your child's school or learning environment, offer to hold a special event or activity at your school, or tell other parents about the great school you have found. Be active and be vocal!

NSCW is designed to be accessible—meaning we want everyone to participate, not just people who work in education. Finally, it is a lot of fun. We even have an official dance and we give people yellow fleece scarves so that they can make the most out of their celebrations and participation. What's not to love about that? Learn more at schoolchoiceweek.com.

paying it forward

AS WE CONCLUDE OUR TIME TOGETHER, I ask you to take a few moments to reflect on where you were at the beginning of this process and where you are now.

I hope that this book has provided you with helpful information, suggestions, ideas, and inspiration that will lead you to finding a school that meets the unique needs of your child. Most importantly, I hope that the advice in this book has reinforced your own intuition as a parent and encouraged you to let your child's needs serve as a roadmap to finding a school or learning environment that works best for your family.

If you have found a school or learning environment that is bringing your child happiness and success, I encourage you to share your experiences with other families. There are so many parents who are ready to embrace the concept of actively choosing an educational environment for their children, but do not know where to start. You can be the spark of inspiration that helps them start their own school choice journey. You can take your child's success and "pay it forward," just like two inspirational parents in Washington, DC did in their own ways.

Years ago, I was assigned to write a feature story for a magazine about a woman who took her own personal struggles and used them to build a movement for positive change in education. That woman is Virginia Walden Ford. From the minute I walked into Virginia's Washington, DC house and sat down for coffee with her, I immediately knew that I had met a friend for life. Little did I know at the time that I would learn more from this woman about working with parents than I would from any other organization or source.

Virginia's story exemplifies the power of school choice. It also perfectly captures the power that each individual parent in our country can have. After seeing her son struggling in school, Virginia found a private scholarship so that he could attend a local Catholic school. Not content to just enjoy his success—he later served our country in the Iraq War and today is a healthy, happy adult—she wanted to make a positive difference for other families who saw their children struggling in school.

At the time, Virginia was a single mother who worked hard make ends meet. But she found the time to build a coalition of other mothers and fathers in the District of Columbia. Together, they successfully lobbied U.S. Congress to pass the

DC Opportunity Scholarship Program, which not only provides K-12 private school scholarships for low-income children but has also increased funding for traditional public schools, public magnet schools, and public charter schools in our nation's capital. Today, tens of thousands of students have benefited from Virginia's work.

Through my work with Virginia, I also met a single father named Joe Kelley. He had four adopted children. Joe's kids struggled in their assigned schools. Once Joe found the scholarship program and identified different schools for each of his kids, his sons and daughters found happiness and success. They loved their schools, and they loved their father.

Years after Joe first discovered the scholarship program, he and his children showed up to every single parent information session, school fair, and application meeting that Virginia planned. They helped with everything from setting up chairs and tables, to passing out information, to helping serve food. Most importantly, though, they told their stories to other families. They offered authentic advice and encouragement to parents who were just learning about the scholarship for the first time.

In 2017, Joe passed away, but his legacy endures in the remarkable children he raised. Virginia's parent empowerment work continues to this very day. To me, both of these parents illustrate so beautifully how neighborhoods, communities, and civil societies are supposed to work. People help people, and together we all rise.

There are so many different ways that you can help families in your own community, even if you only have a fraction of the time that Virginia and Joe spent in their neighborhood. The smallest of actions can make a big difference for another child or another family. If you love the school that your child is attending, tell other parents; thank your child's teachers and the school's principal; share your school choice experiences with other families; celebrate your child's school during National School Choice Week. If you believe that families in your area need and deserve more choices for their children, tell your state lawmakers and help encourage the creation of even more schools in your community or state. In short, try to pay it forward in your own way, just like Virginia and Joe did, and like so many other parents have done before and since.

Our society can only benefit when more families know about the school choice options that are available for children and when more people recognize that these options and choices strengthen our communities, our states, and our nation.

I am enthusiastic and optimistic about the future of education in America. For all of the debate and controversy over different education policies—including school choice—I know that there are millions of talented, inspiring educators and school leaders who are working tirelessly to create school environments that will inspire and motivate students so that they can succeed. These school environments increasingly reflect the diversity and variety we see in communities across the country. Most importantly, the growth in different and unique types of schools means that more children will find schools and learning environments that celebrate their uniqueness and their talents rather than making some students feel uncomfortable, out of place, or irrelevant in their schools or their communities.

I also know that there are tens of millions of students who want to succeed. They have big goals and plans for their futures. They are not jaded. They are eager and optimistic and resilient.

Every child and family have potential. School choice—just like all of the other choices you make for your family—helps that potential rise to the surface. It helps your children reach for the stars. And as parents, the true experts on your children, you are perfectly qualified, capable, and empowered to make these important decisions. In fact, you are the only people who can.

Regardless of the type of school or learning environment you have selected, I sincerely hope that your family's educational journey is filled with happiness and success. You deserve that. Your children deserve that. Our future deserves that.

appendix

In this section, you will find a list of national organizations that provide information about school choice and schools. While this list is comprehensive, it is not exhaustive. Additional resources are available at schoolchoiceroadmap.com, and this list will be updated and augmented on that site. Organizations are listed for reference purposes but do not necessarily reflect an endorsement of all the information contained on the organizations' websites.

Organizations are listed in the following order:

- General Information about K-12 Education
- School Search and Research Resources
- School Organizations by Type and Category
- National School Choice Support and Advocacy Organizations
- School Choice News and Opinion Resources

General Information About K-12 Education

Education Commission of the States
ecs.org

U.S. Department of Education
ed.gov

School Search and Research Resources

Great Schools
greatschools.org

National Center for Education Statistics
nces.ed.gov/ccd/schoolsearch/

National School Choice Week
schoolchoiceweek.com

Niche
niche.com/K12/

Private School Review
privateschoolreview.com

Public School Review
publicschoolreview.com

School Digger
schooldigger.com

School Organizations by Type and Category

ALTERNATIVE EDUCATION
National Alternative Education Association
the-naea.org

ASSEMBLIES OF GOD EDUCATION
League of Christian Schools
lcs.education

BOARDING SCHOOL EDUCATION
The Association of Boarding Schools
boardingschools.com

CATHOLIC EDUCATION
Cristo Rey Network
cristoreynetwork.org

Jesuit Schools Network
jesuitschoolsnetwork.org
National Catholic Educational Association
ncea.org

Office of Lasallian Education at Christian Brothers Conference
lasallian.info

U.S. Conference of Catholic Bishops Office of Education
usccb.org

CHRISTIAN EDUCATION
Association of Christian Schools
actschools.org

Association of Christian Schools International
acsi.org

Christian Schools International
csionline.org

National Christian School Association
nationalchristian.org

Oral Roberts University Educational Fellowship Network
oru.edu

DROPOUT PREVENTION AND RECOVERY
National Dropout Prevention Center
dropoutprevention.org

EPISCOPAL EDUCATION

National Association of Episcopal Schools
episcopalschools.org

Mid-Atlantic Episcopal Schools Association
maesaschools.com

Southwestern Association of Episcopal Schools
swaes.org

FRIENDS/QUAKER EDUCATION

Friends Council on Education
friendscouncil.org

GIFTED AND TALENTED EDUCATION

National Association for Gifted Children
nagc.org

National Society for the Gifted and Talented
nsgt.org

HOMESCHOOLING

Home School Legal Defense Association
hslda.org

Homeschool Now USA
homeschoolnowusa.org

National Home Education Research Institute
nheri.org

INDEPENDENT EDUCATION

National Association of Independent Schools
nais.org

National Independent Private Schools Association
nipsa.org

INTERNATIONAL BACCALAUREATE EDUCATION

International Baccalaureate Schools
ibo.org

ISLAMIC EDUCATION

Council of Islamic Schools in North America
cisnausa.org

Islamic Schools League of America
theisla.org

JEWISH EDUCATION

Agudath Israel of America
agudathisrael.org

Center for Jewish Day Schools (Prizmah)
prizmah.org

Center for Initiatives in Jewish Education
thecije.org

North American Association of Community & Congregational
Hebrew High Schools
naacchhs.org

Orthodox Union
ou.org

JUVENILE JUSTICE EDUCATION

The National Center on Education, Disability, and Juvenile
Justice
edjj.org

The Coalition for Juvenile Justice
juvjustice.org

LABORATORY EDUCATION

International Association of Laboratory Schools
laboratoryschools.org

LANGUAGE IMMERSION EDUCATION

The Association of Two-Way and Dual Language Education
atdle.org

LUTHERAN EDUCATION

Evangelical Lutheran Church in America Education
elca.org/education

Lutheran Church Missouri Synod Education
lcms.org/school-ministry

Lutheran Education
luthed.org

Wisconsin Evangelical Synod Lutheran Schools
wels.net

MENNONITE EDUCATION
Mennonite Schools Council
mennoniteeducation.org

METHODIST EDUCATION
National Association of Schools and Colleges of The United
Methodist Church
gbhem.org

MILITARY EDUCATION
Association of Military Colleges and Schools of the United
States
amcsus.org

MONTESSORI EDUCATION
American Montessori International of the United States
amiusa.org

American Montessori Society
amshq.org

ONLINE SCHOOLS AND BLENDED, DISTANCE, AND DIGITAL LEARNING

Digital Learning Day
digitallearningday.org

Foundation for Blended and Online Learning
blendedandonlinelearning.org

iNACOL
inacol.org

National Coalition for Public School Options
publicschooloptions.org

Online Learning Consortium
onlinelearningconsortium.org

United States Distance Learning Association
usdla.org

Virtual Learning Leadership Alliance
virtuallearningalliance.org

OTHER

Center for Spiritual and Ethical Education
csee.org

PRIVATE SCHOOLS
Council for American Private Education
capenet.org

PROGRESSIVE EDUCATION
Association of Progressive Schools
aops.org

Progressive Education Network
progressiveeducationnetwork.org

PUBLIC CHARTER SCHOOLS
National Alliance for Public Charter Schools
publiccharters.org

National Charter Schools Institute
nationalcharterschools.org

PUBLIC MAGNET SCHOOLS
Magnet Schools of America
magnet.edu

SEMESTER EDUCATION
Semester Schools Network
semesterschools.net

SEVENTH-DAY ADVENTIST EDUCATION
Seventh-day Adventist Board of Education
adventisteducation.org

SINGLE-GENDER EDUCATION
International Boys' Schools Coalition
theibsc.org

The National Coalition of Girls' Schools
ncgs.org

SPECIAL NEEDS EDUCATION
Council for Exceptional Children
cec.sped.org

Federation for Children with Special Needs
fcsn.org

International Association for Special Education
iase.org

Learning Disabilities Association of America
ldaamerica.org

National Association of Private Special Education Centers
napsec.org

National Center for Special Education in Charter Schools
ncsecs.org

Parent Educational Advocacy Training Center
peatc.org

STEM EDUCATION

International STEM Education Association
isea-stem.org

National Consortium of Specialized STEM Schools
ncsss.org

STEM Education Coalition
stemedcoalition.org

TRADITIONAL PUBLIC EDUCATION

American Association of School Administrators
aasa.org

Council of Chief State School Officers
ccsso.org

Council of the Great City Schools
cgcs.org

National Rural Education Association
nrea.net

Small School Districts Association
ssda.org

VOCATIONAL EDUCATION

Association for Career and Technical Education
acteonline.org

International Vocational Education and Training Association
iveta.org

WALDORF EDUCATION

Alliance for Public Waldorf Education
allianceforpublicwaldorfeducation.org

Association of Waldorf Schools of North America
waldorfeducation.org

Research Institute for Waldorf Education
waldorfresearchinstitute.org

National School Choice Support and Advocacy Organizations*

50 State Campaign for Achievement Now (50CAN)
50can.org

American Federation for Children
federationforchildren.org

Center for Education Reform
edreform.com

Center on Reinventing Public Education
crpe.org

Chiefs for Change
chiefsforchange.org

Children's Scholarship Fund
scholarshipfund.org

EdChoice
edchoice.org

Education Reform Now
edreformnow.org

Foundation for Excellence in Education
excelined.org

Home School Legal Defense Association
hslda.org

Homeschool Now USA
homeschoolnowusa.org

Magnet Schools of America
magnet.edu

National Alliance for Public Charter Schools
publiccharters.org

National Coalition for Public School Options
publicschooloptions.org

Policy Innovators in Education Network
pie-network.org

The Thomas B. Fordham Institute
fordhaminstitute.org

Yes Every Kid
yeseverykid.com

School Choice News and Opinion Resources

Choice Media
choicemedia.tv

Education Post
educationpost.org

The 74 Million
the74million.org

*Please note that there are hundreds of organizations that support school choice. The organizations listed in this book are organizations that focus *solely* on education. I take responsibility for any omissions—they were purely accidental. Additional resources are available at schoolchoiceroadmap.com.

bibliography

Advance CTE. "Career Technical Education." Advance CTE. Accessed July 2, 2019. https://careertech.org/cte.

Afterschool Alliance. "What Does the Research Say about Afterschool?," Afterschool Alliance, November 2017. http://afterschoolalliance.org/documents/What_Does_the_Research_Say_About_Afterschool.pdf.

Allen, Jeanne. "The Path to Charter Schools." Center for Education. Reform, June 2019. https://edreform.com/wp-content/uploads/2019/07/CER_Path-to-Charter-Schools_6-2019.pdf.

American Montessori Society. "What Is Montessori Education?" American Montessori Society. Accessed July 2, 2019. https://amshq.org/About-Montessori/What-Is-Montessori.

America's Promise Alliance. "High School Graduation Facts: Ending the Dropout Crisis." America's Promise Alliance, Last updated June 5, 2018. https://www.americaspromise. org/high-school-graduation-facts-ending-dropout-crisis.

Anderson, Cameron. "Respect Matters More Than Money for Happiness in Life." Association for Psychological Science, June 20, 2012. https://www.psychologicalscience.org/news/ releases/respect-from-friends-matters-more-than-money-for-happiness-in-life.html.

Anderson, Michael L., Justin Gallagher, and Elizabeth Ramirez Ritchie. "School Lunch Quality and Academic Performance." NBER Working Paper No. 23218, National Bureau of Economic Research, March 2017. https://www.nber.org/papers/w23218.pdf.

Anderson, Nick. "Useful or foolhardy? New 'adversity rating' for SAT drives rousing debate." *The Washington Post,* May 31, 2019. https://www.washingtonpost.com/local/education/ useful-or-foolhardy-new-adversity-rating-for-sat-drives-rousing-debate/2019/05/31/ c263d528-7afd-11e9-8ede-f4abf521ef17_story.html?utm_term=.7757d38a86e4.

Aravindan, Sudha. "How Diversity Influences Student Achievement." Study.com. Accessed July 2, 2019. https://study.com/academy/lesson/how-diversity-influences-student-achievement.html.

Arkansas State University. "IEPs Are Important Because Special Education Is Important." Arkansas State University, February 22, 2016. https://degree.astate.edu/articles/k-12-education/ieps-are-important-because-special-education-students-are-important.aspx.

ASHA Leader. "Curiosity Associated with Higher Academic Achievement." *ASHA Leader* 23, no. 7 (2018): 14. https://doi.org/10.1044/leader.RIB4.23072018.14.

Association of Military Colleges & Schools of the United States. "Home." Association of Military Colleges & Schools of the United States, 2017. https://amcsus.org/.

Barrington, Kate. "How Does Bullying Affect a Student's Academic Performance?" Public School Review, Last updated May 1, 2018. https://www.publicschoolreview.com/blog/ how-does-bullying-affect-a-students-academic-performance.

Baumert, Jürgen, and Mareike Kunter. "The Effect of Content Knowledge and Pedagogical Content Knowledge on Instructional Quality and Student Achievement." in *Cognitive Activation in the Mathematics Classroom and Professional Competence of Teachers.* Vol. 30. Edited by Mareike Kunter et al., 175–205. Boston: Springer US, 2013.

Beaudoin, Marie-Nathalie. "Respect—Where Do We Start?" *Promoting Respectful Schools* 69, no. 1 (2011): 40–44.

Berry, Michael A. "Healthy School Environment and Enhanced Educational Performance." CIRIscience.org, January 12, 2002. https://www.ciriscience.org/a_314-Healthy-School-Environment-and-Enhanced-Educational-Performance.

Blazer, Christie. "A Review of the Research on Magnet Schools," Miami-Dade County Public Schools, January 2012. https://magnet.edu/files/review-of-research-on-magnet-schools.pdf

Burdick-Will, Julia. "School Violent Crime and Academic Achievement in Chicago." *Sociology of Education* 86, no. 4 (2013): 1–24. https://doi.org/10.1177/0038040713494225.

Burke, Lindsey. "Florida's Universal Education Choice Movement." The Heritage Foundation, February 15, 2019. https://www.heritage.org/education/commentary/floridas-universal-education-choice-moment

Burke, Lindsey. "How School Choice Is Lifting Thousands of Kids Across America." The Heritage Foundation, January 23, 2019. https://www.heritage.org/education/commentary/how-school-choice-lifting-thousands-kids-across-america

Center for Evaluation and Education Policy Analysis. "The Importance of School Facilities in Improving Student Outcomes." Center for Evaluation and Education Policy Analysis, June 7, 2015. https://sites.psu.edu/ceepa/2015/06/07/the-importance-of-school-facilities-in-improving-student-outcomes/.

Center on Education Policy. "Teacher Effectiveness Linked to Student Achievement." Center on Education Policy, January 8, 2013. https://cepr.harvard.edu/news/teacher-effectiveness-linked-student-achievement.

Center for Education Reform. "Building Community Support for Education Reform." Center for Education Reform, December 2009. https://edreform.com/2009/12/building-community-support-for-education-reform-grassroots-action/.

Cheng, Albert, and Paul E. Peterson. "How Satisfied are Parents with Their Children's Schools? New Evidence from a US Department of Education Survey." *Education Next* 17, no. 2 (2017): 20–28.

Cheryan, Sapna, Sianna A. Ziegler, Victoria C. Plaut, and Andrew N. Meltzoff. "Designing Classrooms to Maximize Student Achievement." *Policy Insights from the Behavioral and Brain Sciences* 1, no. 1 (2014): 4–12. https://doi.org/10.1177/2372732214548677.

Chingos, Matthew M., and Grover J. Whitehurst. "Class Size: What Research Says and What it Means for State Policy." Brookings, May 2011. https://www.brookings.edu/research/class-size-what-research-says-and-what-it-means-for-state-policy/.

Chingos, Matthew M., and Martin R. West. "Why Annual Statewide Testing Is Critical to Judging School Quality." Brookings, January 20, 2015. https://www.brookings.edu/research/why-annual-statewide-testing-is-critical-to-judging-school-quality/.

Cimermanová, Ivana. "The Effect of Learning Styles on Academic Achievement in Different Forms of Teaching." *International Journal of Instruction* 11, no. 3 (2018): 219–32. http://files.eric.ed.gov/fulltext/EJ1183439.pdf.

Coalition for Responsible Home Education. "Homeschool Sports Access by State." Coalition for Responsible Home Education, January 30, 2014. https://www.responsiblehomeschooling.org/policy-issues/current-policy/homeschool-sports-access-by-state/.

Coalition for Responsible Home Education. "State Histories of Homeschooling." Coalition for Responsible Home Education. Accessed July 2, 2019. https://www.responsiblehomeschooling.org/histories-of-homeschooling/.

College Board. "Student Participation and Performance in Advanced Placement Rise in Tandem." College Board, Last updated June 2, 2019. https://www.collegeboard.org/releases/2018/student-participation-and-performance-in-ap-rise-in-tandem.

Connections Academy. "Connections Academy Celebrates Prolific Ice Skating Alums Headed to Pyeongchang." Connections Academy, January 29, 2018. https://www.connectionsacademy.com/news/releases/connections-academy-ice-skating-alums.

Cooper, Harris. "Does Homework Improve Academic Achievement?" *Duke Today*, September 23, 2006. https://today.duke.edu/2006/09/homework_oped.html.

Council for American Private Education. "Private School Facts." Council for American Private Education. Accessed July 2, 2019. https://www.capenet.org/facts.html.

Council of Chief State School Officers. "Testing and Opt-Out Provisions in ESSA." CCSSO, July 01, 2019. https://ccsso.org/resource-library/testing-and-opt-out-provisions-essa.

Craft, Steven Wesley. "The Impact of Extracurricular Activities on Student Achievement at the High School Level." University of Southern Mississippi, 2012. https://aquila.usm.edu/cgi/viewcontent.cgi?article=1567&context=dissertations.

Crisis Prevention Institute. "The Case for a Culture of Caring in Schools." Crisis Prevention Institute, March 2018. https://www.crisisprevention.com/Blog/March-2018/The-Case-for-a-Culture-of-Caring-in-Schools.

Dammu, Indira. "Rethinking School Discipline to Support Academic Achievement." SCORE, August 4, 2016. https://tnscore.org/rethinking-school-discipline-to-support-academic-achievement/.

Darling-Hammond, Linda, Robert Rothman, and Peter W. Cookson, Jr. "Expanding High Quality Educational Options for All Students." Learning Policy Institute, December 2017. https://learningpolicyinstitute.org/sites/default/files/product-files/Expanding_High%20Quality_Options_REPORT.pdf.

David, Jane L. "After-School Programs Can Pay off." *Educational Leadership* 68, no. 8 (2011): 84–85.

DeAngelis, Corey. "Setting the Record Straight on School Choice, Charter and Private Schools." Reason Foundation, May 8, 2019. https://reason.org/commentary/setting-the-record-straight-on-school-choice-charter-and-private-schools/

Dervarics, Chuck, and Eileen O'Brien. "Back to School: How Parent Involvement Affects Student Achievement." The Center for Public Instruction. http://www.centerforpubliceducation.org/research/back-school-how-parent-involvement-affects-student-achievement.

DiPerna, Paul and Michael Shaw. "2018 Schooling in America." EdChoice, December 5, 2018. https://www.edchoice.org/research/2018-schooling-in-america-survey/.

EdChoice. "Can I Use a 529 Plan for K–12 Expenses?" EdChoice, March 28, 2018. https://www.edchoice.org/blog/can-i-use-a-529-plan-for-k-12-expenses/.

EdChoice. "School Choice in America Dashboard." EdChoice, Last modified April 9, 2019. https://www.edchoice.org/school-choice/school-choice-in-america/.

EdChoice. "The 123s of School Choice." EdChoice, April 11, 2019. https://www.edchoice.org/research/the-123s-of-school-choice/

EdChoice. "ABCs of School Choice." EdChoice, January 16, 2019. https://www.edchoice.
org/research/the-abcs-of-school-choice/.

Education Commission of the States. "Does the State Have Open Enrollment Programs?"
Education Commission of the States, Last updated October 2018. http://ecs.force.com/
mbdata/MBQuestNB2n?rep=OE1801.

Education Commission of the States. "Advanced Placement: All high schools/districts
required to offer AP?" Education Commission of the States, 2018. http://ecs.force.com/
mbdata/MBQuestRT?Rep=AP0116.

Epstein, Joyce. "Epstein's Six Types of Parent Involvement." FHSD Schools, 2015. https://
www.fhsdschools.org/UserFiles/Servers/Server_995699/File/2015-16/Parents/
Epstein%20-%20Six%20Keys.pdf.

Evergreen Education Group. "Keeping Pace with K–12 Digital Learning Reports." Evergreen
Education Group, 2019. https://www.evergreenedgroup.com/keeping-pace-reports.

ExcelinEd. "The Research on Private Education Choice." ExcelinEd, 2018.

Farris, Michael P. and J. Michael Smith. "State Laws Concerning Participation of Homeschool
Students in Public School Activities." Home School Legal Defense Association,
September 6, 2018. https://hslda.org/content/docs/nche/Issues/E/Equal_Access.pdf.

Families and Schools Together. "The Importance of Parent Engagement: a List of Research
and Thought Leadership." Families and Schools Together, August 25, 2016. https://
www.familiesandschools.org/blog/the-importance-of-parent-engagement/.

Flashman, Jennifer. "Academic Achievement and Its Impact on Friend Dynamics." *Sociology
of Education* 85, no. 1 (2012): 61–80. https://doi.org/10.1177/0038040711417014.

Fletcher, Ben C. "Diversity and Inclusiveness Is Good for Your Well-being." Psychology
Today, September 18, 2016. https://www.psychologytoday.com/us/blog/do-something-
different/201609/diversity-and-inclusiveness-is-good-your-well-being.

FutureEd. "How School Suspensions Affect Student Achievement." FutureEd, September 19,
2018. https://www.future-ed.org/how-school-suspensions-affect-student-achievement/.

Gallagher, Emily. "The Effects of Teacher-Student Relationships: Social and Academic
Outcomes of Low-Income Middle and High School Students." NYU Steinhardt,
December 13, 2013. https://steinhardt.nyu.edu/appsych/opus/issues/2013/fall/gallagher.

Generator School Network. "Service-Learning and Academic Achievement Research Summary." National Youth Leadership Council, 2010. http://www.partnershipsmakeadifference. org/uploads/3/9/3/2/3932381/slresearchsummary.pdf.

Gietz, Carmen, and Kent McIntosh. "Relations Between Student Perceptions of Their School Environment and Academic Achievement." *Canadian Journal of School Psychology* 29, no. 3 (2014): 161–76. https://doi.org/10.1177/0829573514540415.

Godsay, Surbhi. "The Benefits of Volunteering—What We Know." CIRCLE, August 29, 2011. https://civicyouth.org/the-benefits-of-volunteering-%E2%80%93-what-we-know/.

Gonchar, Michael. "Does the Way Your Classroom Is Decorated Affect Your Learning?" *The New York Times*, June 11, 2014. https://learning.blogs.nytimes.com/2014/06/11/does-the-way-your-classroom-is-decorated-affect-your-learning/.

Gorman, Nicole. "Bullying Affects Students' Academic Achievement, Study Finds Education World." Education World, January 31, 2017. https://www.educationworld. com/a_news/bullying-effects-students%E2%80%99-academic-achievement-study-finds-1646296443.

Greene, Jay, Brian Kisida, and Daniel Bowen. "The Educational Value of Field Trips." *Education Next*, 14, no. 1 (2014). https://www.educationnext.org/the-educational-value-of-field-trips/.

Greenspan, Rachel E. "Lori Loughlin and Felicity Huffman's College Admissions Scandal Remains Ongoing. Here Are the Latest Developments." Time, May 15, 2019. https:// time.com/5549921/college-admissions-bribery-scandal/.

Hajovsky, Daniel B., Benjamin A. Mason, and Luke A. McCune. "Teacher-Student Relationship Quality and Academic Achievement in Elementary School: a Longitudinal Examination of Gender Differences." *Journal of School Psychology* 63 (2017): 119–33. http://www.sciencedirect.com/science/article/pii/S0022440517300390.

Hanushek, Eric. "What do test scores really mean for the economy." American Enterprise Institute, June 11, 2018. http://www.aei.org/publication/what-do-test-scores-really-mean-for-the-economy/.

Harris, Jennifer L., Mohammed T. Al-Bataineh, and Adel Al-Bataineh. "One to One Technology and its Effect on Student Academic Achievement and Motivation." *Contemporary Educational Technology* 7, no. 4 (2016): 368–81. https://files.eric.ed.gov/fulltext/EJ1117604.pdf.

Heck, Ronald H. "Teacher Effectiveness and Student Achievement." *Journal of Educational Administration* 47, no. 2 (2009): 227–49. https://doi.org/10.1108/09578230910941066.

Heggart, Keith. "How Important is Subject Matter Knowledge for a Teacher?" EDUtopia, May 1, 2016. https://www.edutopia.org/discussion/how-important-subject-matter-knowledge-teacher.

Helsa, Kevin. "Unified Enrollment Lessons Learned from Across the Country." National Alliance for Public Charter Schools, September 2018. https://www.publiccharters.org/sites/default/files/documents/2018-09/rd3_unified_enrollment_web.pdf.

Hess, Frederick. "How Much Do Rising Test Scores Tell Us About a School?" *Forbes*, September 18, 2018. https://www.forbes.com/sites/frederickhess/2018/09/18/how-much-do-rising-test-scores-tell-us-about-a-school/#4cf4ad2222e8.

Hirsch, Aaron. "The Changing Landscape of Homeschooling in the United States." Center on Reinventing Public Education, July 2019. https://www.crpe.org/publications.

Hitt, Collin, Michael Q. McShane, and Patrick J. Wolf. "Do Impacts on Test Scores Even Matter? Lessons from Long-Run Outcomes in School Choice Research." American Enterprise Institute, March 2018. http://www.aei.org/wp-content/uploads/2018/04/Do-Impacts-on-Test-Scores-Even-Matter.pdf.

Hoff, Jody, and Jane S. Lopus. "Does Student Engagement Affect Student Achievement in High School Economics Classes?" in *The Annual Meetings of the Allied Social Science Association.*, 2014. https://www.frbsf.org/education/files/Does-Student-Engagement-Affect-Student-Achievement-in-High-School-Economics-Classes.pdf.

Home School Legal Defense Association. "Homeschool Laws in Your State." Home School Legal Defense Association. Accessed July 2, 2019. https://hslda.org/content/laws/.

Huseman, Jessica. "Homeschooling Regulations by State." ProPublica, August, 27, 2015. https://projects.propublica.org/graphics/homeschool.

Im, Myung Hee, Jan N. Hughes, Qian Cao, and Oi-Man Kwok. "Effects of Extracurricular Participation During Middle School on Academic Motivation and Achievement at Grade 9." *American Educational Research Journal* 53, no. 5 (2016): 1343–75. https://doi.org/10.3102/0002831216667479.

Individuals with Disabilities Education Act. "IDEA - Home." Individuals with Disabilities Education Act. Accessed July 2, 2019. https://sites.ed.gov/idea/.

International Association of Laboratory Schools. "IALS Membership." International Association of Laboratory Schools. Accessed July 2, 2019. https://www.laboratoryschools. org/membership.

International Baccalaureate Organization. "How IB is different." International Baccalaureate Organization. Accessed July 2, 2019. https://www.ibo.org/benefits/why-the-ib-is-different/.

Jacob, Brian A. "What We Know about Career and Technical Education in High School." Brookings, October 5, 2017. https://www.brookings.edu/research/what-we-know-about-career-and-technical-education-in-high-school/.

Jochim, Ashley, Georgia Heyward, and Betheny Gross. "Fulfilling the Promise of School Choice by Building More Effective Support for Families." Center on Reinventing Public Education, June 2019. https://www.crpe.org/publications/fulfilling-promise-school-choice-building-more-effective-supports-families.

Johnson, Chrystal, and Adrian Thomas. "Caring as Classroom Practice." *Social Studies and the Young Learner* 22, no. 1 (2009): 8–11.

Johnston. "School Cleanliness Affects Student Performance." Johnston, 2017. https://www.johnston.biz/school-cleanliness-affects-student-performance/.

Kaufman, Scott Barry. "Schools Are Missing What Matters About Learning." *The Atlantic*, July 24, 2017. https://www.theatlantic.com/education/archive/2017/07/the-underrated-gift-of-curiosity/534573/.

Koehn, Montie. "Transforming School Culture Through Mutual Respect." Wabisabi Learning, July 14, 2014. https://www.wabisabilearning.com/blog/transforming-school-culture-through-mutual-respect.

Konan, Paul N'Dri, Armand Chatard, Leila Selimbegović, and Gabriel Mugny. "Cultural Diversity in the Classroom and its Effects on Academic Performance." *Social Psychology* 41, no. 4 (2010): 230–37. https://doi.org/10.1027/1864-9335/a000031.

Kulp, Kimberley. "Famous Homeschoolers - Who Are Famous Homeschoolers in History?" Bridgeway Homeschool Academy, February 28, 2019. https://www.homeschoolacademy. com/blog/famous-homeschoolers/.

Ladd, Gary W. "School Bullying Linked to Lower Academic Achievement, Research Finds." American Psychological Association, January 30, 2017. https://www.apa.org/news/press/releases/2017/01/school-bullying.

Ladner, Matthew. "The Next Step in Education Reform." *Education Next* 6 no. 3 (2015). https://www.educationnext.org/the-next-step-in-school-choice-forum-education-savings-accounts/.

Lavy, Victor, and Edith Sand. "The Friends Factor: How Students' Social Networks Affect Their Academic Achievement and Well-Being?" NBER Working Paper 18430, The National Bureau of Economic Research, October 2012. https://www.nber.org/papers/w18430.pdf.

Leedy, Bonnie. "School Communication Strategies and Why Transparency Matters." School Webmasters, September 25, 2018. https://www.schoolwebmasters.com/Blog_Articles?entityid=377765.

Levesque, Karen, Mark Premo, Robert Vergun, David Emanuel, Steven Klein, Robin Henke, Susan Kagehiro, and James Houser. "Key Questions." in *Vocational Education in the United States: The Early 1990s*. https://nces.ed.gov/pubs/web/95024-2.asp.

Lexia Learning. "Grit: An Essential Ingredient of Academic Success." Lexia Learning, March 6, 2017. https://www.lexialearning.com/blog/grit-essential-ingredient-academic-success.

Little, Heather, B. Priscilla, and Christopher B. Wimer. "Afterschool Programs Make a Difference: Findings From the Harvard Family Research Project." *SEDL Letter* 20, no. 2 (August 2008). http://www.sedl.org/pubs/sedl-letter/v20n02/afterschool_findings.html.

Lynch, Matthew. "Examining the Impact of Culture on Academic Performance." The Edadvocate, August 3, 2016. https://www.theedadvocate.org/examining-the-impact-of-culture-on-academic-performance/.

Magnet Schools of America. "A Snapshot of Magnet Schools in America." Magnet Schools of America. Accessed July 2, 2019. https://magnet.edu/resources/research-studies/snapshot-of-magnet-schools-report.

Mathis, William J. "The Effectiveness of Class Size Reduction." National Education Policy Center, June 2016. https://nepc.colorado.edu/sites/default/files/publications/Mathis%20RBOPM-9%20Class%20Size.pdf.

McGaha-Garnett, Valerie. "The Effects of Violence on Academic Progress and Classroom Behavior: From a Parent's Perspective." in *The Annual VISTAS Project: Ideas and Research You Can Use*, Article 91. https://www.counseling.org/docs/default-source/vistas/the-effects-of-violence-on-academic-progress-and-classroom-behavior.pdf?sfvrsn=1828de3f_12.

Midwest Comprehensive Center. "Student Goal Setting: An Evidence-Based Practice." Midwest Comprehensive Center, May 2018. https://midwest-cc.org/sites/default/files/2018-06/MWCC-Student-Goal-Setting-Evidence-Based-Practice-Resource-508.pdf.

Mihaly, Kata. "Do More Friends Mean Better Grades? Student Popularity and Academic Achievement." Working Paper No. 678, RAND Center, March 2009. https://www.rand.org/content/dam/rand/pubs/working_papers/2009/RAND_WR678.pdf.

Mikulecky, Marga Torrence. "Open Enrollment is on the Menu—But Can You Order It?" Education Commission of the States, June 2013. https://www.ecs.org/clearinghouse/01/07/96/10796.pdf

MindShift. "How Important is Grit in Student Achievement?" KQED News, October 2, 2012. https://www.kqed.org/mindshift/24110/how-important-is-grit-in-student-achievement.

Moeller, Aleidine J., Janine M. Theiler, and Chaorong Wu. "Goal Setting and Student Achievement: a Longitudinal Study." *The Modern Language Journal* 96, no. 2 (2012): 153–69. https://doi.org/10.1111/j.1540-4781.2011.01231.x.

Moralez, Justin. "The Time Has Come: A Look at School Choice in Milwaukee." American Federation for Children, November 20, 2017. https://www.federationforchildren.org/the-milwaukee-parental-choice-program/.

Mostafavi, Beata. "Exploring the Link Between Childhood Curiosity and School Achievement." MHealth Lab, April 30, 2018. https://labblog.uofmhealth.org/lab-report/exploring-link-between-childhood-curiosity-and-school-achievement.

National Alliance for Public Charter Schools. "Charter School Datasets: Data Dashboard." National Alliance for Public Charter Schools. Accessed July 2, 2019. https://data.publiccharters.org/.

National Alliance for Public Charter Schools. "Charter School FAQ." National Alliance for Public Charter Schools. Accessed July 2, 2019. https://www.publiccharters.org/about-charter-schools/charter-school-faq.

National Center for Education Statistics. "Characteristics of Traditional Public Schools and Public Charter Schools." National Center for Education Statistics, Last updated May 2019. https://nces.ed.gov/programs/coe/indicator_cla.asp.

National Center for Education Statistics. "Extracurricular Participation and Student Engagement." NCES 95-741, U.S. Department of Education, June 1995. https://nces. ed.gov/pubs95/web/95741.asp.

National Center for Education Statistics. "Fast Facts: Public School Choice Programs." National Center for Education Statistics. Accessed July 1, 2019. https://nces.ed.gov/ fastfacts/display.asp?id=6.

National Center for Education Statistics. "Fast Facts: School Uniforms." National Center for Education Statistics. Accessed July 2, 2019. https://nces.ed.gov/fastfacts/display. asp?id=50.

National Commission on Excellence in Education. "A Nation at Risk: The Imperative for Educational Reform. An Open Letter to the American People." GPO Publication No. 065-000-00177-2, U.S. Government Printing Office, Washington, April 1983. https:// www2.ed.gov/pubs/NatAtRisk/risk.html.

National School Choice Week. "Countdown Begins: National School Choice Week 2019 to Feature 40,000+ Events and Activities Across America." National School Choice Week, January 7, 2019. https://www.prnewswire.com/news-releases/countdown-begins-national-school-choice-week-2019-to-feature-40-000-events-and-activities-across-america-300773843.html.

O'Connor, Megan. "The Importance of Transparency in Education." New York School Talk, January 31, 2018. http://newyorkschooltalk.org/2018/01/importance-transparency-education/.

Office of Innovation and Improvement. "State Regulation of Private and Home Schools." Office of Innovation and Improvement. Accessed July 2, 2019. https://innovation. ed.gov/resources/state-nonpublic-education-regulation-map/.

Office of Planning, Evaluation and Policy Development. "Issue Brief: College-Level Coursework for High School Students." U.S. Department of Education, Washington, April 2017. https://www2.ed.gov/rschstat/eval/high-school/college-level-coursework. pdf.

Office of Special Education and Rehabilitative Services. "Guide to the Individualized Education Program." U.S. Department of Education, July 2000. https://www2.ed.gov/ parents/needs/speced/iepguide/index.html.

Osborne, Charlie. "Parents Want Transparency From Schools Concerning Use of Student Data." ZDnet, January 23, 2014. https://www.zdnet.com/article/parents-want-transparency-from-schools-concerning-use-of-student-data/.

Papadatou-Pastou, Marietta, Maria Gritzali, and Alexia Barrable. "The Learning Styles Educational Neuromyth: Lack of Agreement Between Teachers' Judgments, Self-Assessment, and Students' Intelligence." *Frontiers in Education* 3 (2018): 148. https://doi.org/10.3389/feduc.2018.00105.

Popham, W. James. "Why Standardized Tests Don't Measure Educational Quality." *Educational Leadership* 56, no. 6 (1999): 8–15.

Porter Magee, Marc. "The 50CAN Guide to Building Advocacy Campaigns." 50CAN: The 50-State Campaign for Achievement Now, 2017. https://50can.org/wp-content/uploads/sites/14/2018/10/Guidebook_PDF_download-1.pdf.

Pristine Mind Foundation. "Respect Between Teacher and Student." Pristine Mind Foundation. Accessed July 2, 2019. https://pristinemind.org/library/student-teacher-relationships/.

Privacy Technical Assistance Center. "Transparency Best Practices for Schools and Districts." U.S. Department of Education, July 2014. https://studentprivacy.ed.gov/sites/default/files/resource_document/file/LEA%20Transparency%20Best%20Practices%20final.pdf.

Progressive Education Network. "Our Mission." Progressive Education Network. Accessed July 2, 2019. https://progressiveeducationnetwork.org/mission/.

Raising Special Kids. "Know Your Rights: Students with Disabilities in Charter Schools." Raising Special Kids. Accessed July 2, 2019. https://m.raisingspecialkids.org/resources/education/know-your-rights-students-with-disabilities-in-charter-schools

RAND Corporation. "Teachers Matter: Understanding Teachers' Impact on Student Achievement." RAND, September 2012. https://www.rand.org/pubs/corporate_pubs/CP693z1-2012-09.html.

Rausch, Rita. "Nutrition and Academic Performance in School-Age Children The Relation to Obesity and Food Insufficiency." *Journal of Nutrition & Food Sciences* 03, no. 02 (2013). https://doi.org/10.4172/2155-9600.1000190.

Ray, Brian D. "A Systematic Review of the Empirical Research on Selected Aspects of Homeschooling as a School Choice." *Journal of School Choice* 11, no. 4 (2017): 604–21. https://doi.org/10.1080/15582159.2017.1395638.

Ray, Brian. "Homeschooling Growing: Multiple Data Points Show Increase 2012 to 2016 and Later." National Home Education Research Institute, September 3, 2018. https://www.nheri.org/academic-achievement-homeschool-students/.

Ray, Brian D. "Research Facts on Homeschooling: Homeschool Fast Facts." National Home Education Research Institute, January 7, 2019. https://www.nheri.org/research-facts-on-homeschooling/.

Readiness and Emergency Management for Schools Technical Assistance Center. "Student Perceptions of Safety and Their Impact on Creating a Safe School Environment." Federal Commission on School Safety, 2018. https://rems.ed.gov/docs/Student_Perceptions_Safety_Fact_Sheet_508C.pdf.

Reed, Lora, and Jim Jeremiah. "Student Grit as an Important Ingredient for Academic and Personal Success." *Developments in Business Simulation and Experiential Learning* 44, no. 1 (2017).

Rees, Nina and Andrew Broy. "Study: Charter High Schools Have 7-11% Higher Graduation Rates Than Their Public School Peers." *Forbes*, March 17, 2014. https://www.forbes.com/sites/realspin/2014/03/17/study-charter-high-schools-have-7-11-higher-graduation-rates-than-their-public-school-peers/#18e913b04ff9

Reisteis, Rick. "Is Intellectual Curiosity a Strong Predictor for Academic Performance? | Tomorrow's Professor Postings." Stanford University. Accessed July 2, 2019. https://tomprof.stanford.edu/posting/1278.

Responsive Classroom. "What Research Says About Parent Involvement." Responsive Classroom. Accessed July 2, 2019. https://www.responsiveclassroom.org/what-research-says-about-parent-involvement/.

Sanchez, Claudio. "From A Single Charter School, A Movement Grows." NPR, August 31, 2012. https://www.npr.org/2012/09/02/160409742/from-a-single-charter-school-a-movement-grows.

Schacter, John. "The Impact of Education Technology on Student Achievement: What the Most Current Research Has To Say." Milken Exchange on Education Technology, Santa Monica, 1999. http://www2.gsu.edu/~wwwche/Milken%20report.pdf.

Schaer, Julienne. "The Bare Walls Theory: Do Too Many Classroom Decorations Harm Learning?" NBC News, October 13, 2014. https://www.nbcnews.com/news/education/bare-walls-theory-do-too-many-classroom-decorations-harm-learning-n223436.

Sinha, Nishant. "The Case for Quality Homework: Why it improves learning, and how parents can help -." *Education Next* 19, no. 1 (Winter 2019): 36–43. https://www.educationnext.org/case-for-quality-homework-improves-learning-how-parents-can-help/.

Sinha, Nishant. "Homework, Academic Achievement, and How Much is Too Much? | Emerging Education Technologies." Emerging EdTech, March 13, 2018. https://www.emergingedtech.com/2018/03/homework-higher-academic-achievement-but-not-too-much/.

Tucker, Bill. "Florida's Online Option," *Education Next* 9 no. 3 (Summer 2009). https://www.educationnext.org/floridas-online-option/

Tyner, Adam and Nicholas Munyan-Penney. "Gotta Give 'Em Credit: State and District Variation in Credit Recovery Participation Rates." The Thomas B. Fordham Institute, November 29, 2018. https://fordhaminstitute.org/national/research/gotta-give-em-credit

Umansky, Ilana M., Rachel A. Valentino, and Sean F. Reardon. "The Promise of Bilingual and Dual Immersion Education." CEPA Working Paper No. 15-11, Stanford Center for Education Policy Analysis, Stanford, October 2015. https://cepa.stanford.edu/sites/default/files/wp15-11v201510.pdf.

U.S. Department of Education. "U.S. Department of Education Releases Guidance on Civil Rights of Students with Disabilities." U.S. Department of Education, December 28, 2016. https://www.ed.gov/news/press-releases/us-department-education-releases-guidance-civil-rights-students-disabilities

U.S. News and World Report. "The 2019 Best High Schools." U.S. News and World Report Education, April 30, 2019. https://www.usnews.com/education/best-high-schools.

Véronneau, Marie-Hélène, and Thomas J. Dishion. "Middle School Friendships and Academic Achievement in Early Adolescence: a Longitudinal Analysis." *The Journal of early adolescence* 31, no. 1 (2011): 99–124. https://doi.org/10.1177/0272431610384485.

Walberg, Herbert J. "Standardized Tests Effectively Measure Student Achievement." 2009. https://www.humbleisd.net/cms/lib/TX01001414/Centricity/Domain/5174/Testing%20-%20For.pdf.

Waldorf Education. "Waldorf Education: An Introduction." Waldorf Education. Accessed July 2, 2019. https://www.waldorfeducation.org/waldorf-education.

Waterford. "How Parent Involvement Leads to Student Success." Waterford, November 1, 2018. https://www.waterford.org/education/how-parent-involvment-leads-to-student-success/.

Weisberg, Dan. "Getting Real About Over-Testing." TNTP, March 26, 2015. https://tntp.org/blog/post/getting-real-about-over-testing.

Wexler, Natalie. "Why Homework Doesn't Seem To Boost Learning—And How It Could." *Forbes*, January 3, 2019. https://www.forbes.com/sites/nataliewexler/2019/01/03/why-homework-doesnt-seem-to-boost-learning-and-how-it-could/#7417672d68ab.

Wilder Research. "Nutrition and Students' Academic Performance." Wilder Research, January 2014. https://www.wilder.org/sites/default/files/imports/Cargill_lit_review_1-14.pdf.

Wilson, Mary. "Students' Learning Style Preferences and Teachers' Instructional Strategies: Correlations between Matched Styles and Academic Achievement." *SRATE Journal* 22, no. 1 (2012): 36–44. http://files.eric.ed.gov/fulltext/EJ995172.pdf.

Wing Institute. "What is the Impact of Teacher Instruction on Student Achievement?" Wing Institute. Accessed June 2, 2019. https://www.winginstitute.org/effective-instruction-overview.

Wixom, Micah Ann. "50-State Comparison: Charter School Policies." Education Commission of the States, January 23, 2018. https://www.ecs.org/charter-school-policies/.

Wixom, Micah Ann. "State Homeschool Policies: a Patchwork of Provisions." Education Commission of the States, July 2015. https://www.ecs.org/charter-school-policies/.

Wolpert, Stuart. "Victims of Bullying Suffer Academically as Well, UCLA Psychologists Report." UCLA Newsroom, August 19, 2010. https://newsroom.ucla.edu/releases/victims-of-bullying-suffer-academically-168220.

a note about sources

EXCEPT WHERE INDICATED IN THE ENDNOTES, quotations in this book come from hundreds of individual telephone and online interviews that I conducted with parents and school officials over the course of 2018 and 2019. Each of the individuals quoted in this book consented to my use of portions of their interviews for this work. In some cases, quotations previously appeared in my blog, *Highlighting Happiness,* and are reprinted in this book with the permission of the interview subjects. In some cases, quotations were slightly revised, shortened, or edited for the purposes of clarity.

acknowledgments

I COULD NOT HAVE WRITTEN THIS BOOK without the expertise of the many parents who have shared their stories and experiences with me over the years. I have learned so much by listening to those moms and dads, as well as to their children. They continue to reaffirm my commitment to advancing opportunities in education in any way that I can. To the hundreds of parents who spoke with me for this project, and to those who subsequently allowed me to use their experiences and quotes in this book, I thank you.

Dozens of school leaders and teachers also agreed to be

interviewed for this book. These educational heroes took time out of their busy days to answer my many questions. Through these conversations, I discovered even more diversity and variety in K–12 education—something that I hope I shared effectively in this book. To each of you who talked with me, thank you, and thank you for your commitment to the education and wellbeing of children in the U.S.

When I first started writing this book, I had no idea how many interesting, talented, professional, and truly kind people I would work with throughout the writing and publishing process. Some of these individuals, like Shelby Doyle and Savannah Buckner, are treasured colleagues I have known for quite a while but whose help on this project, from scheduling interviews to marshaling research to editing chapters, was essential. My editor, Holly Rubino from Yellow Bird Editors, was a miracle worker, taking an early version of this manuscript and encouraging me to improve it. My longtime friend, Chris Jacobs, introduced me to the awesome people at Beaufort Books. At Beaufort, the incomparable Megan Trank and Eric Kampmann believed in this project, helped me navigate an unfamiliar process (publishing), and answered my numerous questions—many of which were likely annoying. I am truly honored by and grateful for their support. To the copyeditors at Beaufort Books and Scribendi, thank you for keeping my grammar and punctuation in check and reminding me of the many things I forgot from middle and high school English classes. I am also grateful to Mark Karis for this book's beautiful cover and interior layout.

The entire team at National School Choice Week was immediately supportive of this book, and they encouraged and advised me every step of the way. In particular, I am grateful to Clare Mullin, Sandy Brown, Noelle DeLaney, Randan Steinhauser, Haleigh Madsen, and Julie Collier for not only their help on this project but also for their friendship.

For so many things, and in so many ways both personal and professional, four people will always hold a special place in my heart. To Tracy Gleason, Jeff Robinson, Lisa Graham Keegan, and Virginia Walden Ford, you all are like family to me. Gratitude does not appropriately describe my appreciation and love for you.

Finally, I have been truly blessed in life with a family that has provided me with so many opportunities—opportunities to succeed, to try new things, to learn and discover, to be myself, to make mistakes, to consider different perspectives, and to laugh. I know that not everyone is as lucky as I am—and I am indeed lucky. To my husband, Jason; my mother, Lee; my father, Bob; my brother, Josh; my grandparents; and my extended family: I love you all very, very much.

about the author

ANDREW CAMPANELLA has served as president of National School Choice Week (NSCW) since 2012.

An enthusiastic advocate for opportunities in education, Andrew has led NSCW during a time of remarkable growth. From 150 events and activities in 2011 to more than 40,000 in 2019, NSCW has quickly become the world's largest education-related public awareness effort.

Before joining NSCW, Andrew served as national communications director for the American Federation for Children, where he worked to promote K–12 scholarship programs for low-income children and authored three editions of the School Choice Yearbook. Before that, Andrew served as senior director of teacher recruitment and communications for the American Board for Certification of Teacher Excellence, where he helped recruit 3,500 new teachers for school districts across the country.

Andrew regularly speaks at education and parent empowerment events. His education expertise has been quoted in or featured on CNN, C-SPAN, FOX Business, FoxNews.com, *The Washington Post*, the *Los Angeles Time*s, the *Houston Chronicle*, the *Orlando Sentinel*, and *The Philadelphia Inquirer*, along with thousands of local and regional newspapers, radio stations, television programs, and parenting blogs.

PRNEWS magazine named Andrew the 2015 Event Marketer of the Year. Additionally, Andrew is the author of the 2015 study *Leading the News: 25 Years of Education Coverage*.

Andrew grew up in southern New Jersey and attended traditional public schools from grades K–12. He graduated from American University in Washington, DC, and currently lives in Florida. Andrew will be donating 100% of the proceeds he receives from the sale of this book to raise awareness of opportunities in K-12 education.

Learn more about Andrew at andrewrcamp.com, or follow Andrew on Twitter @andrewrcamp, and/or Facebook at / andrewrcampanella. Andrew does not have an active Instagram account because he has no good pictures to share.

endnotes

1   "Countdown Begins: National School Choice Week 2019 to Feature 40,000+ Events and Activities Across America," National School Choice Week, January 7, 2019, https://www.prnewswire.com/news-releases/countdown-begins-national-school-choice-week-2019-to-feature-40-000-events-and-activities-across-america-300773843.html.

2   "Fast Facts: Public School Choice Programs," National Center for Education Statistics, accessed July 1, 2019, https://nces.ed.gov/fastfacts/display.asp?id=6.

3   Marga Torrence Mikulecky, "Open Enrollment is on the Menu–But Can You Order It?," Education Commission of the States, June 2013, https://www.ecs.org/clearinghouse/01/07/96/10796.pdf; Nina Rees and Andrew Broy, "Study: Charter High Schools Have 7-11% Higher Graduation Rates Than Their Public School Peers," *Forbes*, March 17, 2014, https://www.forbes.com/sites/realspin/2014/03/17/study-charter-high-schools-have-7-11-higher-graduation-rates-than-their-public-school-peers/#18e913b04ff9; Christie Blazer, "A Review of the Research on Magnet

Schools," Miami-Dade County Public Schools, January 2012, https://magnet. edu/files/review-of-research-on-magnet-schools.pdf; "The Research on Private Education Choice," ExcelinEd, 2018.

4   "Fast Facts: Public School Choice Programs," National Center for Education Statistics, accessed July 1, 2019, https://nces.ed.gov/fastfacts/display.asp?id=6; "High School Graduation Facts: Ending the Dropout Crisis," America's Promise Alliance, Last updated June 5, 2018, https://www.americaspromise.org/high-school-graduation-facts-ending-dropout-crisis.

5   "Fast Facts: Public School Choice Programs," National Center for Education Statistics, accessed July 1, 2019, https://nces.ed.gov/fastfacts/display.asp?id=6.

6   National Commission on Excellence in Education, "A Nation at Risk: The Imperative for Educational Reform. An Open Letter to the American People." GPO Publication No. 065-000-00177-2 (U.S. Government Printing Office, Washington, 1983), https://www2.ed.gov/pubs/NatAtRisk/risk.html.

7   Claudio Sanchez, "From A Single Charter School, A Movement Grows," NPR, August 31, 2012, https://www.npr.org/2012/09/02/160409742/from-a-single-charter-school-a-movement-grows.

8   Justin Moralez, "The Time Has Come: A Look at School Choice in Milwaukee," American Federation for Children, November 20, 2017, https://www. federationforchildren.org/the-milwaukee-parental-choice-program/.

9   "Charter School Datasets: Data Dashboard," National Alliance for Public Charter Schools, accessed July 2, 2019, https://data.publiccharters.org/.

10   "ABCs of School Choice," EdChoice, January 16, 2019, https://www.edchoice.org/research/the-abcs-of-school-choice/.

11   "Does the State Have Open Enrollment Programs?," Education Commission of the States, Last updated October 2018, http://ecs.force.com/mbdata/MBQuestNB2n?rep=OE1801.

12   Bill Tucker, "Florida's Online Option," Education Next, Summer 2009, vol. 9 no. 3, https://www.educationnext.org/floridas-online-option/.

13   "Keeping Pace with K–12 Digital Learning Reports," Evergreen Education Group, 2019, https://www.evergreenedgroup.com/keeping-pace-reports.

14   "State Histories of Homeschooling," Coalition for Responsible Home Education, accessed July 2, 2019, https://www.responsiblehomeschooling.org/histories-of-homeschooling/.

15   Brian D. Ray, "Homeschooling Growing: Multiple Data Points Show Increase 2012 to 2016 and Later," National Home Education Research Institute, September 3, 2018, https://www.nheri.org/academic-achievement-homeschool-students/.

16   "Characteristics of Traditional Public Schools and Public Charter Schools," National Center for Education Statistics, Last updated May 2019, https://nces.ed.gov/programs/coe/indicator_cla.asp.

17   "Does the State Have Open Enrollment Programs?," Education Commission of the States, Last updated October 2018, http://ecs.force.com/mbdata/ MBQuestNB2n?rep=OE1801.

18   "DeZavala Elementary School," GreatSchools.org, accessed July 2, 2019, https:// www.greatschools.org/texas/houston/3385-De-Zavala-Elementary-School/.

19   "Advanced Placement: All high schools/districts required to offer AP," Education Commission of the States, 2018, http://ecs.force.com/mbdata/ MBQuestRT?Rep=AP0116.

20   Office of Planning, Evaluation and Policy Development, "Issue Brief: College-Level Coursework for High School Students" (U.S. Department of Education, Washington, 2017), https://www2.ed.gov/rschstat/eval/high-school/college-level-coursework.pdf.

21   "Student Participation and Performance in Advanced Placement Rise in Tandem," College Board, Last updated June 2, 2019, https://www.collegeboard.org/ releases/2018/student-participation-and-performance-in-ap-rise-in-tandem.

22   "Burbank Middle School Earns Seven Distinction Designations," Houston Independent School District, 2019, https://www.houstonisd.org/domain/38442.

23   "Burbank Middle School," GreatSchools.org, accessed July 2, 2019, https://www. greatschools.org/texas/houston/3366-Burbank-Middle-School/.

24   Ibid

25   "Charter School Datasets: Data Dashboard," National Alliance for Public Charter Schools, accessed July 2, 2019, https://data.publiccharters.org/.

26   Ibid

27   "Charter School FAQ," National Alliance for Public Charter Schools, accessed July 2, 2019, https://www.publiccharters.org/about-charter-schools/charter-school-faq.

28   Micah A. Wixom, "50-State Comparison: Charter School Policies," Education Commission of the States, January 23, 2018, https://www.ecs.org/charter-school-policies/.

29   "Cologne Academy," GreatSchools.org, accessed July 2, 2019, https://www. greatschools.org/minnesota/cologne/5555-Cologne-Academy/

30   "A Snapshot of Magnet Schools in America," Magnet Schools of America, accessed July 2, 2019, https://magnet.edu/resources/research-studies/snapshot-of-magnet-schools-report

31   Ibid

32   Ibid

33   Ibid

34   "Academic Magnet High School," US News and World Report Education, April 30, 2019, https://www.usnews.com/education/best-high-schools/south-carolina/districts/ charleston-county-school-district/academic-magnet-high-school-17566.

35   Ibid

36   "Spring Hill High School," US News and World Report Education, April 30, 2019, https://www.usnews.com/education/best-high-schools/south-carolina/districts/ lexington-05/spring-hill-high-147615.

37 "Magnet Schools of America Announces 2018 Award Winners," Magnet Schools of America, April 2018, https://magnet.edu/magnet-schools-of-america-announces-first-cohort-of-nationally-certified-magnet-schools-3-2.

38 "Keeping Pace with K–12 Digital Learning Reports," Evergreen Education Group, 2019, https://www.evergreenedgroup.com/keeping-pace-reports.

39 Ibid

40 "Connections Academy Celebrates Prolific Ice Skating Alums Headed to PyeongChang," Connections Academy, January 29, 2018, https://www.connectionsacademy.com/news/releases/connections-academy-ice-skating-alums.

41 "Private School Facts," Council for American Private Education, accessed July 2, 2019, https://www.capenet.org/facts.html.

42 "School Choice in America Dashboard," EdChoice, Last modified April 9, 2019, https://www.edchoice.org/school-choice/school-choice-in-america/.

43 Ibid

44 "State Regulation of Private and Home Schools," Office of Innovation and Improvement, accessed July 2, 2019, https://innovation.ed.gov/resources/state-nonpublic-education-regulation-map/.

45 Ibid

46 Ibid

47 "School Choice in America Dashboard," EdChoice, Last modified April 9, 2019, https://www.edchoice.org/school-choice/school-choice-in-america/.

48 "Homeschool Laws in Your State," Home School Legal Defense Association, accessed July 2, 2019, https://hslda.org/content/laws/.

49 Jessica Huseman, "Homeschooling Regulations by State," ProPublica, August, 27, 2015, https://projects.propublica.org/graphics/homeschool.

50 Michael P. Farris and J. Michael Smith, "State Laws Concerning Participation of Homeschool Students in Public School Activities," Home School Legal Defense Association, September 6, 2018, https://hslda.org/content/docs/nche/Issues/E/Equal_Access.pdf; "Homeschool Sports Access by State," Coalition for Responsible Home Education, January 30, 2014, https://www.responsiblehomeschooling.org/policy-issues/current-policy/homeschool-sports-access-by-state/;

51 Ibid

52 Brian D. Ray, "Research Facts on Homeschooling: Homeschool Fast Facts," National Home Education Research Institute, January 7, 2019, https://www.nheri.org/research-facts-on-homeschooling/.

53 Kimberley Kulp, "Famous Homeschoolers - Who Are Famous Homeschoolers in History?," Bridgeway Homeschool Academy, February 28, 2019, https://www.homeschoolacademy.com/blog/famous-homeschoolers/.

54 Brian D. Ray, "A Systematic Review of the Empirical Research on Selected Aspects of Homeschooling as a School Choice," *Journal of School Choice* 11, no. 4 (2017), https://doi.org/10.1080/15582159.2017.1395638.

55   "Homeschool Laws in Your State," Home School Legal Defense Association, accessed July 2, 2019, https://hslda.org/content/laws/.

56   Micah A. Wixom, "State Homeschool Policies: A Patchwork of Provisions," Education Commission of the States, July 2015, https://www.ecs.org/charter-school-policies/.

57   Jessica Huseman, "Homeschooling Regulations by State," ProPublica, August, 27, 2015, https://projects.propublica.org/graphics/homeschool.

58   Coalition for Responsible Home Education, "Homeschool Sports Access by State," January 30, 2014, https://www.responsiblehomeschooling.org/policy-issues/current-policy/homeschool-sports-access-by-state/.

59   "Career Technical Education," Advance CTE, accessed July 2, 2019, https://careertech.org/cte.

60   "How IB is different," International Baccalaureate Organization, accessed July 2, 2019, https://www.ibo.org/benefits/why-the-ib-is-different/.

61   "IALS Membership," International Association of Laboratory Schools, accessed July 2, 2019, https://www.laboratoryschools.org/membership.

62   Ilana M. Umansky, Rachel A. Valentino, and Sean F. Reardon, "The Promise of Bilingual and Dual Immersion Education" CEPA Working Paper No. 15-11 (Stanford Center for Education Policy Analysis, Stanford, 2015), https://cepa.stanford.edu/sites/default/files/wp15-11v201510.pdf.

63   "Home," Association of Military Colleges & Schools of the United States, 2017, https://amcsus.org/.

64   "What Is Montessori Education?," American Montessori Society, accessed July 2, 2019, https://amshq.org/About-Montessori/What-Is-Montessori.

65   "Our Mission," Progressive Education Network, accessed July 2, 2019, https://progressiveeducationnetwork.org/mission/.

66   Karen Levesque et al., "Key Questions," in Vocational Education in the United States: The Early 1990s, https://nces.ed.gov/pubs/web/95024-2.asp.

67   "Waldorf Education: An Introduction," Waldorf Education, accessed July 2, 2019, https://www.waldorfeducation.org/waldorf-education.

68   "Dr. T.J. Owens Gilroy Early College Academy," US News and World Report Education, April 30, 2019, https://www.usnews.com/education/best-high-schools/california/districts/gilroy-unified/dr-t-j-owens-gilroy-early-college-academy-2271.

69   "IDEA - Home," Individuals with Disabilities Education Act, accessed July 2, 2019, https://sites.ed.gov/idea/

70   "U.S. Department of Education Releases Guidance on Civil Rights of Students with Disabilities," U.S. Department of Education, December 28, 2016, https://www.ed.gov/news/press-releases/us-department-education-releases-guidance-civil-rights-students-disabilities.

71   "Know Your Rights: Students with Disabilities in Charter Schools," Raising Special Kids, accessed July 2, 2019, https://m.raisingspecialkids.org/resources/education/know-your-rights-students-with-disabilities-in-charter-schools

72   "Fast Facts: School Uniforms," National Center for Education Statistics, accessed July 2, 2019, https://nces.ed.gov/fastfacts/display.asp?id=50

73   "Can I Use a 529 Plan for K–12 Expenses?," EdChoice, March 28, 2018, https://www.edchoice.org/blog/can-i-use-a-529-plan-for-k-12-expenses/

74   "Homeschool Sports Access by State," Coalition for Responsible Home Education, January 30, 2014, https://www.responsiblehomeschooling.org/policy-issues/current-policy/homeschool-sports-access-by-state/.

75   Rachel E. Greenspan, "Lori Loughlin and Felicity Huffman's College Admissions Scandal Remains Ongoing. Here Are the Latest Developments," *Time*, May 15, 2019, https://time.com/5549921/college-admissions-bribery-scandal/.

76   Nick Anderson, "Useful or foolhardy? New 'adversity rating' for SAT drives rousing debate," *The Washington Post*, May 31, 2019, https://www.washingtonpost.com/local/education/useful-or-foolhardy-new-adversity-rating-for-sat-drives-rousing-debate/2019/05/31/c263d528-7afd-11e9-8ede-f4abf521ef17_story.html?utm_term=.7757d38a86e4.

77   Ibid